Identity Unknown

Imagine being unable to recognise your spouse, your children, or even yourself when you look in the mirror, despite having good eyesight and being able to read well and name objects. This is a condition that, in rare cases, some brain injury survivors experience every day.

Identity Unknown gives an exceptional, poignant and in-depth understanding of what it is like to live with the severe after-effects of brain damage caused by a viral infection of the brain. It tells the story of Claire, a nurse, wife and mother of four, who, having survived encephalitis, was left with an inability to recognise faces—a condition also known as prosopagnosia—together with a loss of knowledge of people and a more general loss of semantic memory.

Part I describes our current knowledge of encephalitis, of perception and memory, and the theoretical aspects of prosopagnosia, semantic memory and sense of self and self-identity. Part II, told in Claire's own words, is an account of her life before her illness, her memories of the early days in hospital, an account of the treatment she received at the Oliver Zangwill Centre, and her description of the long-term consequences of encephalitis. Claire's profound insights, clear writing style and powerful portrayal of her feelings provide us with a moving insider's view of prosopagnosia. These chapters also contain additional commentary from Barbara Wilson and Claire's husband Ed, providing further detail about the condition, treatment possibilities, potential outcomes and follow-up options.

Identity Unknown provides a unique personal insight into a condition that many of us have, for too long, known too little about. It will be of great interest to a broad audience, including professionals working in rehabilitation settings and all those who have sustained a brain injury, their families ar

Barbara A. Wilson is a neuropsychologist and founder of the Oliver Zangwill Centre for Neuropsychological Rehabilitation in Ely, UK. She has worked in brain injury rehabilitation for over 35 years and has published 21 books, 270 journal articles and chapters and 8 neuropsychological tests. Among her many awards she has an OBE and two lifetime achievement awards. She is the editor of the journal *Neuropsychological Rehabilitation*, which she founded in 1991.

Claire Robertson is a nurse, mother, wife and friend. She qualified as a State Registered Nurse, a Sick Children's nurse and a nurse for Special and Intensive Care of the Newborn. She survived Herpes simplex encephalitis in 2004, which left her with a very severe loss of knowledge of people and their identity. She regularly gives talks about her difficulties and the experience of life after brain injury.

Joe Mole is a psychology assistant at the Oliver Zangwill Centre for Neuropsychological Rehabilitation in Ely, UK. He is currently involved in research into the neuropsychology of face recognition, navigation and time perception.

After Brain Injury: Survivor Stories
Series Editor: Barbara A. Wilson

This new series of books is aimed at those who have suffered a brain injury, and their families and carers. Each book focuses on a different condition, such as face blindness, amnesia and neglect, or diagnosis, such as encephalitis and locked-in syndrome, resulting from brain injury. Readers will learn about life before the brain injury, the early days of diagnosis, the effects of the brain injury, the process of rehabilitation, and life now. Alongside this personal perspective, professional commentary is also provided by a specialist in neuropsychological rehabilitation, making the books relevant for professionals working in rehabilitation, such as psychologists, speech and language therapists, occupational therapists, social workers and rehabilitation doctors. They will also appeal to clinical psychology trainees and undergraduate and graduate students in neuropsychology, rehabilitation science and related courses who value the case study approach.

With this series, we also hope to help expand awareness of brain injury and its consequences. The World Health Organisation has recently acknowledged the need to raise the profile of mental health issues (with the WHO Mental Health Action Plan 2013–20) and we believe there needs to be a similar focus on psychological, neurological and behavioural issues caused by brain disorder, and a deeper understanding of the importance of rehabilitation support. Giving a voice to these survivors of brain injury is a step in the right direction.

Published titles:

Life After Brain Injury
Survivors' stories
By Barbara A. Wilson, Jill Winegardner, Fiona Ashworth

Identity Unknown
How acute brain disease can destroy knowledge of oneself and others
By Barbara A. Wilson, Claire Robertson, Joe Mole

Identity Unknown

How acute brain disease
can destroy knowledge of
oneself and others

Barbara A. Wilson,
Claire Robertson
and Joe Mole

 **Psychology Press**
Taylor & Francis Group

LONDON AND NEW YORK

First published 2015
by Psychology Press
27 Church Road, Hove, East Sussex BN3 2FA

and by Psychology Press
711 Third Avenue, New York, NY 10017

Psychology Press is an imprint of the Taylor & Francis Group, an informa business

British Library Cataloguing in Publication Data
A catalogue record for this book is available from the British Library

Library of Congress Cataloging in Publication Data
Wilson, Barbara A., 1941-
Identity unknown : how acute brain disease can destroy knowledge of oneself
and others / Barbara A. Wilson, Claire Robertson, and Joe Mole.
pages cm. — (After brain injury)
Includes bibliographical references and index.
1. Robertson, Claire—Health. 2. Encephalitis—Patients—Biography.
3. Brain damage—Patients--Rehabilitation—Biography. 4. Brain
damage—Patients—Biography. I. Robertson, Claire, 1961- II.
Mole, Joe (Joseph Alexander), 1988- III. Title.
RC390.W55 2015
616.8'3200092—dc23
[B]
2014018507

ISBN: 978-1-84872-284-2 (hbk)
ISBN: 978-1-84872-285-9 (pbk)
ISBN: 978-1-315-76271-5 (ebk)

Typeset in Times New Roman
by Swales & Willis Ltd, Exeter, Devon, UK

MIX
Paper from responsible sources
FSC FSC® C013056
www.fsc.org

Printed and bound in Great Britain by
TJ International Ltd, Padstow, Cornwall

Contents

Illustrations

Figures

Tables

Series preface

After Brain Injury: Survivor Stories was launched in 2014 to meet the need for a series of books aimed at those who have suffered a brain injury, and their families and carers. Brain disorders can be life-changing events with far-reaching consequences. However, in the current climate of cuts in funding and service provision for neuropsychological rehabilitation, there is a risk that people whose lives have been transformed by brain injury are left feeling isolated, with little support.

So many of the books on brain injury are written for academics and clinicians and filled with technical jargon, so are of little help to those directly affected. Instead, this series offers a much-needed personal insight into the experience, as each book is written by a survivor, or group of survivors, who are living with the very real consequences of brain injury. Each book focuses on a different condition, such as face blindness, amnesia and neglect, or diagnosis, such as encephalitis and locked-in syndrome, resulting from brain injury. Readers will learn about life before the brain injury, the early days of diagnosis, the effects of the brain injury, the process of rehabilitation and life now.

Alongside this personal perspective, professional commentary is also provided by a specialist in neuropsychological rehabilitation. The historical context, neurological state of the art, and data on the condition, including the treatment, outcome and follow-up, will also make these books appealing for professionals working in rehabilitation, such as psychologists, speech and language therapists, occupational therapists, social workers and rehabilitation doctors. They will also be of interest to clinical psychology trainees and undergraduate and graduate students in neuropsychology, rehabilitation science and related courses who value the case study approach as a complement to the more academic books on brain injury.

With this series, we also hope to help expand awareness of brain injury and its consequences. The World Health Organisation has recently acknowledged the need to raise the profile of mental health issues (with the WHO Mental Health Action Plan 2013–20) and we believe there needs to be a similar focus on psychological, neurological and behavioural issues arising from brain disorder, accompanied by a deeper understanding of rehabilitation support. In giving a voice to survivors of brain injury in this series we hope to raise awareness of the consequences of brain injury and how some of them might be alleviated through rehabilitation in which therapists, patients and their families work together.

Barbara A. Wilson

Foreword

Dr Bonnie-Kate Dewar

In 2004, I was asked to conduct a neuropsychological assessment at Addenbrookes Hospital, Cambridge, on a woman recovering from encephalitis—Claire. At the time I was working as a clinical neuropsychologist with Professor Barbara Wilson, in the MRC Cognition and Brain Sciences Unit Cambridge, a role that included occasional clinical sessions with Dr Narinder Kapur, Clinical Neuropsychologist at Addenbrookes. Looking back now to my initial meeting with Claire, I have a patchy memory of a small table in a clinic room taking note of some unusual responses to a standard naming test as her semantic memory deficits were revealed. What could have been a typical encounter for a clinical neuropsychologist of a few hours of assessment, and possibly some feedback, evolved into a relationship that was to support Claire across years in her quest to try to make sense of the multiplicity of changes thrust upon her by the viral encephalitis.

Claire's story, here in this book, is prefaced by an introduction to the neuropsychological consequences of encephalitis. As with other forms of acquired brain injury, the neuropsychological deficits and impairments secondary to encephalitis will differ from person to person. Following the episode of Herpes simplex viral encephalitis, Claire experienced and continues to experience face blindness—prosopagnosia. Barbara Wilson and Joe Mole provide a thorough and fulsome summary of current understanding of agnosias, notably face blindness, and the routes of face recognition. The encephalitis also caused significant impairments in Claire's memory, both semantic and autobiographical, interrupting her understanding of who she is, her personal history and story, and of her place in the world. Claire's words move the focus from the impact of the prosopagnosia and other cognitive deficits at an intellectual level to an understanding of the impact upon her everyday functioning and participation.

This book tells Claire's journey in her words, the words of her family and also of the rehabilitation therapists who worked alongside her. Her poignant and honest recollections highlight the need for psychologists, clinicians, doctors and therapists to listen to and hear the voices of the patients that we assess and treat if we are to have a greater empathy with our clients and develop appropriate rehabilitation supports. As one of her treating clinicians, it is interesting and humbling to receive her feedback—what helped, what didn't and how difficult it is to re-learn face and person-specific knowledge in the clinic, let alone the challenge of generalisation to everyday life. A narrow focus on face re-training does not adopt the necessary holistic framework to address the whirl-wind of change that occurred for Claire within her roles as mother, wife and friend. We were able to take some steps together to understand her anxiety and how to understand her identity post-encephalitis, and I must acknowledge the excellent clinical supervision I received in my work with Claire from Dr Fergus Gracey, Clinical Psychologist, at the time based at the Oliver Zangwill Centre. Claire's story demonstrates the power of the therapeutic relationship and the hope we need to give to our clients to explore possibilities in a psychologically safe and understand-ing place.

The most striking theme to emerge from Claire's story is the discon-nection between her past identity and how she experiences herself fol-lowing the encephalitis. She not only describes an ongoing struggle with face and person identification, but also the discord between who people think she is and the confused "muddle" she finds herself in following the encephalitis. Claire's anchor points for her identity have been wrenched away by the encephalitis—with an inability to remember past relation-ships and experiences with friends and family—and she becomes, in her own words, "a stranger to myself". She describes those elements that defined her—wife, mum, nurse and friend—as lost or changed. Instead, she is left with a yearning to remember and reclaim herself—to be an "am" and not a "was". The reader becomes aware of those elements of memory that define self, including relationships, and how these must necessarily be changed following acquired brain injury. As rehabilitation therapists/specialists we may talk of acceptance and adjustment; Claire's story highlights the long and difficult journey towards adjustment that many of our clients with acquired brain injury may experience. Her story is infinitely richer than additional, yet valuable, information gleaned from a standardised outcome questionnaire.

Our memories tell our story. We are defined by the people around us and our memories of those relationships. I first met Claire in 2004 and continue to have intermittent contact with her through the Encephalitis Society (www.encephalitis.info). She cannot recognise my face. She knows me by name and it is always with great warmth and excitement that I am recognised. My clinical work continues to be informed by my relationship with Claire—of what is helpful in memory rehabilitation, of the power of hope and of humour in the rehabilitation journey, and the role I have in helping people to put back the jigsaw of their identity following acquired brain injury, with the likely inclusion of a few new pieces along the way.

Dr Bonnie-Kate Dewar
Clinical Neuropsychologist
March 2014

Preface

Imagine being unable to recognise your spouse, your children or even yourself when you look in the mirror, despite having good eyesight and being able to read well and name objects. This is a condition that Claire, a wife, mother and former nurse, experiences every day. She survived a brain illness, encephalitis, in 2004. It did not affect her physical ability, her language or her basic vision, but left her with face blindness, also known as prosopagnosia. Not only is she unable to recognise faces, she has lost most of the information about people she once knew well. She has also lost many of her memories about herself and feels she is no longer the person she once was. This book tells her story, how she copes with her vastly changed life and how she maintains her independence.

In general, there is a lack of understanding of the life-changing consequences of brain injury. Subsequently, the crucial importance of rehabilitation for survivors is very far from being recognised. By providing the reader with a deeper understanding of what it is like to live with the severe consequences of brain damage caused by a viral infection of the brain, from both a personal and a professional viewpoint, we hope that the reader will recognise the value of rehabilitation and see that it is possible for a person whose brain has been injured to lead a full and meaningful life, despite persisting effects of impairment. Although Claire, the protagonist and co-author of this book, is sometimes in despair at what happened to her, she nevertheless feels that on many occasions she is coping well with the problems that confront her in daily life. While anxiety is rarely far away, Claire is learning to accept her changed life and is able to say: "This is how I am now, we have one life—so live it."

Part I of the book consists of four chapters by Barbara Wilson and Joe Mole, in which they discuss our current knowledge of encephalitis and many of its consequences, including prosopagnosia and identity loss. These early chapters offer a resumé of historical and contemporary research and current knowledge, which it is hoped will serve as a theoretical underpinning for the reader to fully appreciate Claire's story, as told in Part II, when she describes her daily battle with the consequences of prosopagnosia. Both parts of the book contain discussion on the kinds of rehabilitation offered to people with brain injury. In Part I, this is continuous and professionally informed, whereas in Part II it is there as an occasional addition or extension to clarify some aspect of Claire's discussion of personal experiences. Part II is the core of the book, consisting in the main of Claire's narration of her life before the illness; her memories of the early days in hospital; an account of the treatment she received at the Oliver Zangwill Centre; and her description of the long-term consequences of encephalitis. Her story offers a unique report on daily living with a condition about which, for too long, too little has been known. Summaries of Claire's preliminary assessment and her rehabilitation at the Oliver Zangwill Centre are provided in the Appendices for those readers who wish to know more detail about her time at the Centre.

Chapter 1 discusses encephalitis, its low rate of occurrence and its effects, which can have variable and sometimes extreme consequences. Chapter 2 discusses perceptual deficits including prosopagnosia, known also as "face blindness". What kind of brain damage causes it, what is its nature, can recovery be expected, and what kinds of treatment have been offered to people with this condition? The third chapter offers a more detailed account of prosopagnosia, including theoretical perspectives of this rare condition. Chapter 4 considers how we understand the sense of self and why this might be affected by brain injury. These four chapters are written by Barbara Wilson, a clinical neuropsychologist, and Joe Mole, an assistant psychologist.

The bedrock of the book, however, is written by Claire herself, with some contributions and comments interspersed throughout from Barbara and Claire's husband Ed. Claire chronicles her early life before the illness struck; she describes the effects of her illness, the early days in hospital, her rehabilitation and her daily life as it is now lived. Claire's profound insights and her considerable ability to portray her feelings in a clear and coherent writing style provide us with a poignant and fascinating insider's view of prosopagnosia. Her story also illustrates the effects and value of the rehabilitation she received for her emotional and cognitive problems and her own willingness to engage and profit from the process.

A NOTE TO READERS: If you are unfamiliar with academic research into problems associated with encephalitis and more specifically prosopagnosia and loss of semantic and autobiographical memory, you may prefer to go straight to Claire's story in Part II and then return to Part I as a follow-up. Those familiar with research into these areas may prefer to read the book in chronological order. There are also two appendices: Appendix 1, which summarises Claire's assessment, and Appendix 2, which details the rehabilitation programme offered to Claire at the Oliver Zangwill Centre. These can be read at any time to confirm sections of the story Claire is telling or they, too, can be left until Claire's story is completed.

Acknowledgements

I (Claire Robertson) would like to acknowledge and hugely thank every single one of the enormous number of people who have kindly and lovingly been there for me, throughout this time of troubles. I don't wish to single anyone out, as you have all been individually very special—family, friends and therapists; without your patience, caring and long ears, I wouldn't be the Claire I am today. You all know who you are, please remind me sometime! Warmest thanks to all of you, Claire x

Barbara A. Wilson and Joe Mole would like to thank Karalyn Patterson, Mick Wilson, Jill Winegardner and Tamara Ownsworth for reading and commenting on the manuscript and for their very helpful suggestions; Rosaleen McCarthy for providing us with her test materials; Jessica Fish for her generous help in tracking down references; the staff at the Oliver Zangwill Centre for their help with Claire's rehabilitation and for permission to include summaries of Claire's reports, especially Sue Brentnall, Leyla Prince, Fergus Gracey, Siobhan Palmer, Andrew Bateman, Kate Psaila, Donna Malley, Jacqui Cooper, Jo Cope and Juliette O'Dell; Ed for agreeing to be interviewed; Fergus Gracey, again, for his discussions and advice; Lizzie Doherr for supporting Claire following her discharge from the Oliver Zangwill Centre; Dr James Rowe and Dr Timothy Rittman of Addenbrooke's Hospital for their help with Claire's scan; Graham and Annie Mole for their suggestions regarding the manuscript; Bede Smith for his invaluable support; Lucy Kennedy and Michael Fenton from Psychology Press for their encouragement in completing this book; Psychology Press for permission to reproduce the formulation model in Appendix 2 from Dewar & Gracey (2007) ("Am not was": Cognitive-behavioural therapy for adjustment and identity change following *Herpes simplex* encephalitis, in Dewar, B.-K. & Williams, W. H. (Eds.), *Encephalitis: Assessment and Rehabilitation Across the Lifespan: Neuropsychological Rehabilitation Special Issue*, 17, 602–620) and for permission to reproduce two figures from Ownsworth (2014) (*Self-Identity After Brain Injury*. Hove: Psychology Press); Informa Healthcare for permission to reproduce a figure from Douglas (2013) (Conceptualizing self and maintaining social connection following severe traumatic brain injury. *Brain Injury*, 27, 60–74); and to all the other people who have made this book possible. Finally, we would like to acknowledge the huge contribution to the theoretical understanding of person recognition made by The Bruce and Young Model of 1986.

Part I

Chapter 1

Encephalitis

What is encephalitis and how common is it?

Encephalitis simply means an inflammation of the brain (Granerod & Crowcroft, 2007). There are two major types of encephalitis. The first is caused by an infection from a virus, bacteria or a parasite, whereas the second results from an abnormal immune response in which the body attacks itself (Stone & Hawkins, 2007) and can be triggered by a recent infection or vaccination (ibid.). The most common infections, at least in the Western world, are those caused by the Herpes simplex virus (the same virus that causes the common cold sore) and Varicella zoster (the virus that causes chicken pox and shingles). Measles, mumps and cyto-megalovirus are examples of other viruses that can cause inflammation of the brain. In other parts of the world, West Nile virus, Japanese virus and viruses from the bites of ticks or mosquitoes may be the cause (Stone & Hawkins, 2007; Stapley, Atkins, & Easton, 2009). Frequently, indeed in more than 50% of cases, the infecting virus cannot be determined (Granerod & Crowcroft, 2007; Stapley et al., 2009).

Of the non-infectious encephalopathies, inflammation of the brain is caused by the central nervous system attacking itself. Acute dissemi-nated encephalomyelitis (ADEM) is an acute demyelinating condition that mainly affects children and young adults. One study showed that it was triggered by an infectious illness or vaccination in 74% of cases (Stone & Hawkins, 2007). This happened to Kate, a young teacher, who developed a sore throat and an influenza-type illness. After a few days she lost consciousness and was later diagnosed with ADEM. Although physically handicapped, Kate was cognitively unimpaired. She describes her journey and her slow but continuing improvement over a 14-year period in a book of survivors' stories by Wilson and Bainbridge (2013).

There are, of course, other kinds of autoimmune encephalopathies. One rare and recently identified autoimmune form is anti-NMDA receptor encephalitis, where NMDA stands for *N*-methyl-D-aspartate. This is an acute form of encephalitis, potentially lethal but with a high probability of recovery, which is caused by an autoimmune reaction. An excellent book, written by a survivor of this form of encephalitis, was recently published (Cahalan, 2012). Susannah Cahalan was a successful young reporter (aged 24 years) for the *New York Post* when she started to become unwell with strange symptoms. She became worse and began to experience hallucinations, paranoia and seizures. One diagnosis from the medical profession concluded that she was having a breakdown caused by stress, while another suggested it was symptoms of withdrawal due to alcoholism. Continuously deteriorating, Susannah became extremely thin, was hospitalised, and came close to being admitted to a long-stay psychiatric unit. She was then fortunate enough to be seen by a Syrian-born psychiatrist, Dr Najjar. He gave her the classic "clock" test, usually administered by neuropsychologists, which indicated that she had unilateral neglect (most often associated with a right hemisphere stroke). In other words, Susannah had organic damage to her brain. She then had to undergo a biopsy, which revealed that her brain was inflamed, caused by cells from her immune system attacking nerve cells in her brain. Four years earlier, Dr Dalmau (from Pennsylvania) had identified a rare type of autoimmune encephalitis, NMDA autoimmune encephalitis. Susannah became the 217th person in the world to be diagnosed with this rare disorder. Treatment began and she slowly improved to the extent that she eventually returned to work, and now continues to be a brilliant journalist and gifted speaker. Most professionals involved in the treatment of Susannah before her final diagnosis thought her illness was due to stress or emotional difficulties, so, sadly, she was not referred for neuropsychological assessment, which would have detected signs of organic brain damage much earlier.

For many people, encephalitis begins with an influenza-type illness or headache, followed, hours or days later, by more serious symptoms, which can include a drop in the level of consciousness (ranging from mild confusion to coma), high temperature, seizures, sensitivity to light and other changes in behaviour. As Stapley and colleagues (2009) state, the types of symptoms seen in encephalitis reflect the specific areas of the brain affected by inflammation. The range of possible symptoms and their rate of development vary widely, thus making it difficult to actually diagnose encephalitis. Granerod and Crowcroft (2007) provide a good review of the epidemiology of encephalitis, while Stone and Hawkins (2007) deliver a comprehensive medical review.

Stone and Hawkins (2007) estimate that, in the USA alone, one in a million people each year contract Herpes simplex viral encephalitis

(HSVE), while Leake and colleagues (2004) suggest that the incidence of ADEM is 0.4–0.8 per 100,000 population per year. Looking at all cases, the Patient.co.uk website (www.patient.co.uk) reports that there are around 4000 cases of encephalitis each year in the UK, with infections being seen most frequently and most severely in children and the elderly. Hokkanen and Launes (2007) state that 20,000 cases occur each year in the USA. However, a recent paper by Granerod, Cousens, Davies, Crowcroft, and Thomas (2013) suggests that the incidence is higher than has been thought. The only previous study looking at the incidence in the UK (Davison, Crowcroft, Ramsay, Brown, & Andrews, 2003) reported 1.5 cases per 100,000 population per year for viral encephalitis alone. However, as most cases are of unknown aetiology and an increasing number of viruses are known to cause the condition, this was felt to be a serious underestimate. Furthermore, many cases are not reported, despite the fact that encephalitis is a notifiable disease in the UK.

Granerod and colleagues (2013) carried out an exhaustive investigation of hospital records to estimate the number of encephalitis cases in England "attributable to infectious and noninfectious causes" (p. 1455). They found an incidence rate of 5.23 cases per 100,000 population per year. The incidence rate was highest among patients less than one year of age and over 65 years of age. Females were 8% less likely to contract the disease than males. This paper is recommended for those interested in the incidence of encephalitis.

Compared to other infectious diseases, encephalitis has a high mortality rate. Some 10% of those with encephalitis die from their infections or from complications resulting from a secondary infection. Some forms of encephalitis have more severe outcomes, including Herpes encephalitis, for which the mortality is 15–20% with treatment and 70–80% without treatment (Stapley et al., 2009).

Help for survivors and their families, as well as for those who have lost a loved one, is provided by the Encephalitis Society (see the section "The Encephalitis Society" later in this chapter and www.encephalitis. info). For parents, siblings and grandchildren who have been bereaved, another source of assistance is the support group The Compassionate Friends (www.tcf.org.uk).

The neuropsychological consequences of encephalitis

A host of cognitive, emotional and psychosocial problems are faced by survivors of encephalitis (Kapur et al., 1994; Hokkanen, Salonen, &

Launes, 1996; Hokkanen & Launes, 2007; Pewter, Williams, Haslam, & Kay, 2007). Details of the neuropsychological assessments of 19 survivors, with various forms of encephalitis, are presented in the paper by Pewter *et al.* (2007). For the purposes of this book, however, we focus on the neuropsychological consequences of HSVE, first because it is the most common kind seen in the Western world, and second because it is the viral encephalitis that Claire endured. The virus tends to attack the temporal lobes, the orbitofrontal cortices and the limbic system. For this reason, memory and executive problems are common (Stapley *et al.*, 2009). Some people, of course, suffer very mild effects from the illness, or none at all, while others are left with devastating deficits and handicaps. Pewter *et al.* (2007) report that memory deficits are the most common cognitive problems experienced, with a high percentage of survivors also showing impairments of executive functioning. These latter issues include difficulties with planning, organisation, problem solving and divided attention. Hooper, Williams, Wall, and Chua (2007) noticed that executive deficits in children are also associated with higher levels of parental stress.

One of the best-known survivors of HSVE in the UK is Clive Wearing (Wilson, Baddeley, & Kapur, 1995; Wilson, 1999; Wearing, 2005; Wilson, Kopelman, & Kapur, 2008). Clive, a professional musician, conductor and world expert on the Renaissance composer Orlando Lassus, became ill with HSVE in March 1985. He has one of the most severe cases of amnesia on record; he cannot retain information for more than a few seconds, he cannot learn new information, and he has lost much of the knowledge about his earlier life. Thus, he has both anterograde and retrograde amnesia. Here, it is debated as to whether it is possible to have one without the other, but most people with anterograde amnesia have some retrograde amnesia. Retrograde amnesia without anterograde amnesia is a much rarer condition. Nevertheless, it has been documented in patients with HSVE (O'Connor, Butters, Militois, Eslinger, & Cermak, 1992; Fujii, Yamadori, Endo, Suzuki, & Fukatsu, 1999; Tanaka, Miyazawa, Hashimoto, Nakano, & Obayashi, 1999). Hokkanen and Launes (2007) provide a more detailed discussion of memory problems following HSVE.

In addition to memory deficits, executive problems are also reported, which include difficulties with planning, organisation, problem solving and divided attention. In one study by Utley *et al.* (1997), 9 of 22 HSVE patients had persistent executive impairments. Pewter and colleagues (2007) report that up to 84% of their sample showed problems in tests of executive functioning. Language problems, typically anomia (i.e. a naming deficit), are frequently experienced (Benjamin *et al.*, 2007). Category-specific semantic deficits may also be seen, where people are much better able to recognise one category of objects than another. Commonly, they have a disproportionate problem recognising living things compared to non-living things (Warrington & Shallice, 1984). Two of the patients in the Warrington and Shallice study, JBR and SBY, both of whom had sustained HSVE, showed "a striking discrepancy between their ability to identify inanimate objects either with pictures or words and their inability to identify living things. J.B.R. was almost at ceiling level on the visual inanimate object condition, yet he virtually failed to score on the visual living things condition" (p. 837). JBR is the same patient as Jason, described in Wilson (1999), who showed the same discrepancy when asked to draw objects. He was able to produce good drawings of a bicycle and an aeroplane, for example, but could not draw a recognisable fish or bird. The opposite pattern is less often seen but does occur. Sacchett and Humphreys (1992) report a stroke patient who was better with living things than manufactured objects, and Laws and Sartori (2005) describe the same phenomenon in a patient with HSVE.

Acquired disorders of reading are also seen after encephalitis (Kapur *et al.*, 1994). Indeed, Jason, in addition to his problems with recognising living objects, also had a surface dyslexia, which means errors in reading aloud words, with an atypical correspondence between spelling and sound (e.g. pronouncing the written word "sew" to rhyme with "new", "few", "chew" and so on). Clive, too, had a mild form of this disorder (Wilson, 1999). Perceptual problems, including agnosia (failure to recognise objects) and prosopagnosia (face blindness) are also seen, but these will be addressed in Chapter 2. Suffice it to say here that Pewter *et al.* (2007) administered two perceptual tests (the Object Decision and Cube Analysis subtests) from the Visual Object and Space Perception Battery (Warrington & James, 1991) and found that 32% of patients failed the Object Decision subtest and 5% the Cube Analysis subtest.

As well as cognitive problems resulting from HSVE, there can be emotional, psychosocial and behavioural difficulties (Pewter *et al.*, 2007; Stapley *et al.*, 2009). A large-scale survey of members carried out by the Encephalitis Society (Dowell, Easton, & Solomon, 2000) found that 68% reported frustration and anger, 67% anxiety, 59% mood swings and 58% depression. Pewter and colleagues (2007), in order to measure psychiatric distress, administered the Revised Symptom Checklist 90 (Derogatis, 1983) to 37 post-encephalitic patients (not all with HSVE), and found that 10 of the 11 indices were elevated in their sample. Only paranoid ideation remained within normal limits. Participants scored highest on the obsessive-compulsive, depression, phobic anxiety and global severity indices. In children, of course, educational problems are most likely to be part of the picture. Starza-Smith, Talbot, and Grant (2007), working in a service for children, said that 80% of their referrals were for behavioural and educational concerns.

Thus, survivors of encephalitis face numerous problems, ranging from cognitive to emotional, behavioural and psychosocial. While help and support is provided by the Encephalitis Society, as discussed in the final section of this chapter, there is substantial evidence that structured rehabilitation, organised by professionals (unfortunately, very thin on the ground owing to a lack of appreciation, understanding and funding), helps people to understand and come to terms with their problems.

Neuropsychological rehabilitation for survivors of encephalitis

Neuropsychological rehabilitation is concerned with the amelioration of cognitive, emotional, psychosocial and behavioural deficits caused by an insult to the brain (Wilson, Evans, Gracey, & Bateman, 2009). It is recognised that these deficits are interlinked and all should be targeted in rehabilitation. There are a number of books on rehabilitation for those who have survived neurological insults and, although these are mostly concerned with survivors of traumatic brain injury (TBI) and stroke, the principles apply across all kinds of acquired brain injury. Prigatano (1999) provides us with general principles of neuropsychological rehabilitation. Wilson (2009) focuses on memory therapy, and Wilson et al. (2009) discuss the holistic approach taken at the Oliver Zangwill Centre for Neuropsychological Rehabilitation. Klonoff (2010) offers a very readable account of psychotherapy after brain injury, and Wilson, Winegardner, and Ashworth (2013), working in combination with the survivors of brain injury and their families, tell the stories of 17 survivors of brain injury and their journey through rehabilitation. Claire, herself, is one of the survivors who contributed to this book.

A special issue of the journal *Neuropsychological Rehabilitation* (edited by B.-K. Dewar and W. H. Williams, 2007) is of particular relevance here as it concentrates on "Encephalitis: Assessment and rehabilitation across the lifespan". The issue contains reports on several rehabilitation studies aimed at reducing the problems faced by people with HSVE, as well as their families. Starza-Smith et al. (2007) describe the treatment of three children, and four papers discuss rehabilitation with adults, three of whom had memory disorders. Miotto (2007) helped a man to learn the names of people and to improve his recall of verbal information, while Emslie, Wilson, Quirk, Evans, and Watson (2007) used a paging system to increase independence in four survivors of encephalitis (three of whom had HSVE). Berry and colleagues (2007) describe SenseCam, a small wearable camera that was used to improve autobiographical memory in a 63-year-old woman diagnosed with limbic encephalitis (one of the autoimmune encephalopathies).

The final paper in the Dewar and Williams (2007) special issue is a report of Claire's rehabilitation, in which she received cognitive behavioural therapy (CBT) to help her adjust to anxiety and identity changes caused by the HSVE (Dewar & Gracey, 2007). Claire was known as VO in this paper. The assessment of her emotional adjustment, mood and behaviour found that she was anxious and tearful and felt overwhelmed in everyday situations. She said her mood was low, she felt hopeless and she had lost interest in the future. Her symptoms were not severe enough to warrant a diagnosis of major depression, but she met the criteria for a generalised anxiety disorder. The CBT given to Claire started with education and the development of a therapeutic relationship. She was then taught to monitor her emotional responses and identify negative thoughts. She learned relaxation techniques to manage her anxiety and was helped to manage her problems with memory, fatigue and loss of identity.

Identity issues are currently very important in brain injury rehabilitation and are addressed by Gracey and Ownsworth (2008) and in a new book by Ownsworth (2014). The problems Claire faced with these issues are tackled in later sections of this book.

The Encephalitis Society

The Encephalitis Society began life as the "Encephalitis Support Group" and was founded by Elaine Dowell, whose son had survived encephalitis and was left with cognitive and behavioural problems. When I (Barbara Wilson) saw my first patient with encephalitis in 1979, I was perfectly able to carry out a neuropsychological assessment and help the team plan a rehabilitation programme. There was no support for families, however, and through my work, I knew only too well the devastating effects this illness can have on them, as well as the immediately affected individual. In 1994 I heard about the support group from Elaine Dowell and began to interact with Elaine at meetings. For many years Elaine was the main spokesperson for this society, and she saw it grow from a small group of parents of children who had survived this illness to a flourishing society encompassing parents, neurologists, neuropsychologists, psychiatrists, occupational therapists, speech and language therapists and, of course, survivors themselves. This group became a society in 2004 and now holds its own conferences, produces literature to help families and professionals, and funds research. Ava Easton joined the society in 2000 and has shown passion and flair in her pursuit of its aims. Without the tireless and innovative commitment of Elaine and Ava, it is unlikely that this society would have survived or grown to its present level. Before the society was established in 1994, there was almost nowhere for families to go for information, advice and support. Now, it is the first port of call for them and also, in many cases, for professionals. Elaine and Ava have played a very large part in setting up the society, ensuring its progress over the years, seeing it through the transition from support group to a society, and bringing together survivors, families and professionals. They are true pioneers as well as conscientious and admirable allies of all those who have survived encephalitis and those involved in the care of people with encephalitis. Elaine retired in 2012, so Ava, the chief executive officer, is the main spokesperson. Of course there are other people behind the scenes who have also played large parts in ensuring the success of the society.

In summary, education, advice and support are provided by the Encephalitis Society to survivors, families and professionals. Its website is www.encephalitis.info.

Chapter 2

An introduction to visual perceptual disorders and to the agnosias

Perception

Barry (2011) said that "One of the most important functions of our brain is to integrate the information from all our senses into a perceptual whole. Only then can we perceive the world as single, integrated and stable, allowing us to move through it moulding it to our needs and desires" (p. vii).

Perception is the process of integrating information we receive from our senses, or, in other words, making sense of what we see, hear, touch, smell or taste. Adequate sensory functioning is a prerequisite for normal perception, but impairment at the sensory level cannot be described as a perceptual problem. We would not, therefore, regard a blind person as having a visual perceptual deficit or a deaf person as having an auditory perceptual problem. Instead, we recognise that they have sensory impairments. It is, of course, possible for sensory and perceptual difficulties to coexist, but we cannot assess perceptual abilities when severe sensory impairment exists in the same modality. Kartsounis (2010) distinguishes between early visual processing disorders and higher visual recognition disorders. Among the former are problems recognising differences in size or shape. Among the latter are problems recognising objects, colours and faces.

In 1992, Goodale and Milner proposed the two-streams hypothesis. They believe that we possess two distinct visual systems, which follow two main pathways or "streams". One is for knowing *what* things are (the ventral stream), and the other is for knowing *where* things are (the dorsal stream). The *what* (ventral) stream travels to the temporal lobe and the *where* (dorsal) stream to the parietal lobe. The former is involved with object identification and recognition, and the latter processes the object's spatial location relevant to the viewer. In 1997, Wilson, Clare, Young, and Hodges published a paper supporting this distinction. They compared two men of the same age, one with HSVE who knew *where* things were but not what they were, and the other with sustained anoxic damage who knew *what* things were but not where they were.

A helpful classification of visual perceptual disorders is provided by ffytche, Blom, and Catani (2010). Visual perceptual and visual spatial deficits are common following brain injury, and neuropsychologists regularly measure such functioning. Groh-Bordin and Kerkoff (2010) suggest that 30% of stroke patients and 50% of TBI patients have such difficulties. Pewter and colleagues (2007), as we saw in the last chapter, found that 32% of survivors of encephalitis failed the Object Decision subtest of the Visual Object and Space Perception Battery (Warrington & James, 1991). These patients may, for example, be unable to discriminate overlapping figures or be unable to recognise objects when seen from an unusual angle. In one survey of perceptual problems following TBI, McKenna *et al.* (2006) found significantly higher incidences of agnosia, unilateral neglect, impairments in body schema and constructional skills in the TBI sample compared to the normative sample. No significant relationship was found between the presence of visual perceptual impairments and the level of cognitive and functional impairment after TBI. The most common impairments were related to unilateral neglect (a failure to report, respond or attend to stimuli on one side of space), with over 45% of patients showing signs of this. This was followed by impairments of body schema, a term used to describe the representation of the positions of body parts in space (Zoltan, 2007), with almost 29% of patients showing signs of this disorder. The third most common disorder was with constructional skills, and was experienced by almost 26% of patients.

It is not only patients with TBI, of course, who are faced with perceptual problems. They are common after stroke, encephalitis and hypoxic brain damage. Far less common are the agnosias, that is to say problems recognising objects and faces. Zihl and Kennard (1996) suggest that these probably occur in fewer than 1% of all neurological cases but, as we shall see in Chapter 3, they may be more prevalent than previously expected.

The agnosias

Visual object agnosia

Visual object agnosia is the inability to recognise objects despite adequate eyesight and naming ability or, as Teuber (1968) stated, it is "A normal percept stripped of its meaning". If we are going to diagnose someone with agnosia we need to ensure that the inability to recognise object is not due to poor vision or a naming difficulty, or to poor comprehension of what is expected. Patients can typically recognise an object through the auditory modality. Jenny, for example, described in Wilson (1999), was unable to recognise a matchbox. When shown one, she said it was a playing card box. When the matchbox was shaken, however, she knew immediately what it was. Jenny was also good at naming to description, so when asked what is the name of a vegetable that we chop up, use in stews and makes your eyes water, she could say straight away that it was an onion. When she saw an onion, however, she thought it was a ball or an apple. She could see and copy small objects, some as small as two millimetres in height, so she had no acuity problems, she just could not recognise what she was seeing.

Although there is no consistently agreed taxonomy of the agnosias (Farah, 2004), one distinction that is widely used, and seems to have empirical validation, is between associative and apperceptive agnosia (Lissauer, 1890). People with apperceptive agnosia cannot draw or match to sample, they cannot point to objects named by the examiner, and their behaviour suggests severe visual difficulties. Objects, faces, letters and shapes can be affected. Visual stimuli may drop out of awareness because of abnormal fatigability. Such individuals suffer from simultanagnosia, which is an inability to see more than one object at a time, or they can only see one part of an object, making it difficult or impossible to recognise objects (Zoltan, 2007). Paula, for example, one of the patients described in Wilson (1999), could only see one part of an object shown to her. Thus, when shown a drawing of a kangaroo, Paula saw the tail on one occasion and a leg on another. When shown a drawing of a thimble above a finger she said "It's white and bumpy, it must be a cauliflower"; she did not perceive the finger at all. This kind of agnosia is associated with bilateral posterior lesions.

People with associative agnosia, on the other hand, are able to copy and match to sample, indicating that they are not in any sense blind. Difficulties with faces, colours and words may also be present, although this does not always occur. As mentioned above, auditory recognition is intact in these individuals, but their tactile recognition may or may not be complete. Those with intact tactile recognition may have a disconnection syndrome, while those with impaired tactile recognition are thought to have a visual semantic memory deficit (Davidoff & Wilson, 1985; Wilson & Davidoff, 1993). While most patients with associative agnosia have bilateral occipitotemporal lesions, other lesion sites, including unilateral lesions, may also result in this disorder (Farah, 2004). Both kinds are rare, but apperceptive agnosia is even rarer than associative agnosia.

There are other types of agnosia, including topographical agnosia (an inability to find one's way around familiar environments), agnosia for letters (or word blindness), verbal auditory agnosia (or word deafness), colour agnosia (or the inability to recognise colours) and simultanagnosia (or the inability to see two things at the same time). For further information on these disorders see Humphreys and Riddoch (1987), Farah (2004), Zihl (2011), Zoltan (2007), Coslett and Saffran (1992) and Hanley and Kay (2010).

Prosopagnosia

Prosopagnosia, also known as face blindness, is the inability to recognise faces, despite apparently intact visual recognition of other stimuli and intact intellectual functioning (Farah 2004). The term "prosopagnosia" was coined by Bodamer in 1947, from the Greek words *prosopon*, meaning "face", and *agnosia*, meaning "not knowing". Perhaps the first description of difficulty with faces after suspected brain injury can be found as far back as in the writings of the Greek general Thucydides (Thucydides II, 47–50), where he describes the behaviour of plague survivors (De Haan, 1999).

Some references to the phenomenon from the middle of the nineteenth century can be found in the neurological literature (Jackson, 1876; Wigan, 1844; Quaglino, Borelli, Della Sala, & Young, 2003) and possibly even in Lewis Carroll's (1871) "Through the looking-glass and what Alice found there" where we find the following dialogue between Alice and Humpty Dumpty:

> "Good-bye, till we meet again!" she said as cheerfully as she could.
>
> "I shouldn't know you again if we did meet," Humpty Dumpty replied in a discontented tone, giving her one of his fingers to shake: "you're so exactly like other people."
>
> "The face is what one goes by, generally," Alice remarked in a thoughtful tone.
>
> "That's just what I complain of," said Humpty Dumpty. "Your face is the same as everybody else has—the two eyes, so—" (marking their places in the air with his thumb) "nose in the middle, mouth under. It's always the same. Now if you had the two eyes on the same side of the nose, for instance—or the mouth at the top—that would be some help."
>
> Quoted by Larner (2004)

Faces are important to us. Newborn babies prefer to look at faces rather than other objects. Even though faces are very similar to one another, most of us recognise our family, friends, colleagues and people on television, without effort. Maurer, Le Grand, and Mondloch (2002) observe "Adults are experts at recognizing faces: they can recognize thousands of individuals at a glance, even at a distance, in poor lighting, with a new hairdo, after 10 years of ageing, or when the face is seen from a novel viewpoint" (p. 255).

As Bruce and Young (1998) reported, people with prosopagnosia know when they are looking at a face, but lose all sense of who it might be. Often, they can see the individual features, indicate if it is a man or woman, or if the person is young or old, and even judge accurately the person's emotional expression. However, in severe cases, they may fail to recognise even the most familiar faces, such as their children, their spouses and even themselves (Zoltan, 2007).

In an influential model on understanding face recognition, Bruce and Young (1986) propose that every face we know is associated with its own recognition unit and that this recognition unit must be activated if we are to access semantic information about the person. Failure to activate the appropriate recognition unit will lead to a known face being deemed unfamiliar. Failure to access semantic information will produce the state in which a perceiver finds a face familiar but cannot remember to whom it belongs (Hanley, Young, & Pearson, 1989) This model is further explored in Chapter 3.

Thus, we can classify people with prosopagnosia into those who can recognise people by their voice or name, and those who have impaired semantic memory for people and cannot recognise them from their face, voice or name. A good account of a patient with this difficulty following temporal lobe epilepsy is provided by Ellis, Young, and Critchley (1989). Gainotti (2013) states ". . . [In] patients with right anterior temporal lobe (ATL) lesions (and sparing of the occipital and fusiform face areas), who present a defect of familiar people recognition, with normal results on tests of face perception, the disorder is often multimodal, affecting voices (and to a lesser extent names) in addition to faces" (p. 99). This is true of Claire, who did, indeed, have right ATL damage (as we describe later). However, she also had some involvement of the fusiform area.

The deficit in face recognition is sometimes strikingly complete. As Farah (2004) states, "most people with visual object agnosia can recognise some objects under some conditions". However, this is not so with someone like Claire, who cannot recognise a single face reliably. Farah describes one patient who saw a man walking towards him behaving strangely; he then realised he was walking towards a mirror and the strange man was himself. Claire also describes this happening to her (Wilson & Claire, 2013).

Some people with prosopagnosia have problems recognising other objects, and even those with no visual object agnosia may have problems distinguishing between similar objects such as the makes of cars (De Haan, Young, & Newcombe, 1987) or birds, as in the case of an ornithologist (Bornstein, 1963). In contrast, a man studied by McNeil and Warrington (1993) developed prosopagnosia after a series of strokes. He then became a sheep farmer and learned to recognise the faces of his sheep, despite the fact that he could not recognise human faces. This kind of evidence suggests that there is something special about human faces, and that prosopagnosia is not simply a problem in recognising or discriminating between within-category stimuli (Farah, 2004). Farah (2004) describes an experiment in which a man with prosopagnosia was required to discriminate between human faces and an equivalent number of very similar stimuli from the same category, namely eye-glass frames. He was disproportionately impaired on the human faces.

Until the mid-1970s it was thought that prosopagnosia could only be caused by brain injury or neurological illness. It is now apparent that this is far from the case (Behrmann & Avidan, 2005; Behrmann, Avidan, Marotta, & Kimchi, 2005; DeGutis, Bentin, Robertson, & D'Esposito, 2007; Duchaine, Yovel, Butterworth, & Nakayama, 2006; LeGrand *et al.*, 2006; McConachie, 1976). Prosopagnosia can be developmental and often hereditary (Behrmann *et al.*, 2005; Duchaine, 2003; Duchaine, Germine, & Nakayama, 2007; Kennerknecht *et al.*, 2006; Kennerknecht, Ho, & Wong, 2008; Schmalzl, Palermo, & Coltheart, 2008a). The only difference between developmental and congenital prosopagnosia appears to be that the latter is hereditary. Duchaine and colleagues (2007) described one family in which congenital prosopagnosia affected ten members. Combined, developmental and congenital prosopagnosias appear to affect 2.5% of the Caucasian population (Kennerknecht *et al.*, 2006; Duchaine, 2008). Cases of prosopagnosia after injury, or acquired prosopagnosia, are also not as rare as once thought. In our own experience, difficulty with faces seems to be a common consequence of brain injury. Recent research has found that, when tested, 21% of 100 brain-injured patients had prosopagnosia (Valentine, Powell, Davidoff, Letson, & Greenwood, 2006). However, despite its apparently high prevalence, and known psychosocial consequences (Bornstein, 1963; Yardley, McDermott, Pisarski, Duchaine, & Nakayama, 2008; Fine, 2011), we still know surprisingly little about how best to treat face blindness.

Because faces are so important to humans, large areas of the brain are involved in face recognition (Bruce & Young, 1998). Some parts are more involved in determining an individual's identity and others in interpreting emotion. Although prosopagnosia can occur after lesions in different parts of the brain, the temporal lobes seem to be crucially involved (Bruce & Young, 1998) and Farah (2004) states that a right hemisphere lesion is essential. Some believe that bilateral involvement is required (Damasio, Damasio, & Van Hoesen, 1982), while others believe it can occur after damage to the right hemisphere alone (De Renzi, 1986a; Zoltan, 2007). Barton, Press, Keenan, and O'Connor (2002) state that face blindness is associated with medial occipitotemporal lesions, especially on the right. Functional imaging has revealed a focal region in the right fusiform gyrus activated specifically during face perception. A very recent review by Rossion (2014) suggests that a unilateral right hemisphere lesion is sufficient to cause prosopagnosia. It is also necessary, unless the patient is left-handed. There are five cases reported of prosopagnosia associated with a unilateral left hemisphere lesion; of these, four are left-handed and one is an ambiguous case.

Claire underwent magnetic resonance imaging (MRI) two years after she developed encephalitis (see Figure 2.1). The scan indicated extensive right anteromedial temporal lobe damage, including damage to the entorhinal and perirhinal cortices, amygdala and hippocampus. The damage extended posteriorly, but with some intact posterior inferior temporal lobe. There was also damage to the left anteromedial temporal lobe including the perirhinal cortex, with some involvement of the

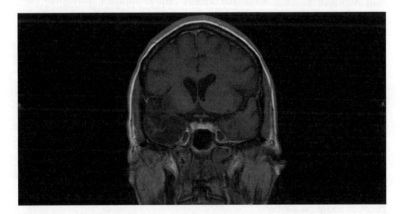

Figure 2.1 Claire's MRI scan, conducted two years post-illness.

fusiform gyrus. The left hippocampus appeared relatively intact along the anterior posterior axis.

Recovery from agnosia

As pointed out by Zihl (2011), there are few accounts of recovery from visual object agnosia or from prosopagnosia. Adler (1944) described a patient who became agnosic following carbon monoxide poisoning sustained in a fire in the USA. In 1950 Adler reported that she had made only minimal recovery after five years. Interestingly, the woman was followed up 40 years later (Sparr, Jay, Drislane, & Venna, 1991); she still had visual object agnosia together with prosopagnosia, alexia, impaired imagery and spatial disorientation. Anoxic brain damage may lead to some very severe problems (Wilson, 1997, 1999). More recovery is sometimes seen after TBI. Kertesz (1979), for more than 10 years, followed up a patient who became agnosic after a road traffic accident; the patient showed no significant recovery. In contrast, Wilson and Davidoff (1993) also followed up, for 10 years, a patient who had sustained a TBI in a horse-riding accident who showed some recovery, particularly for real objects, although she still had problems with animals and other stimuli. This is the same patient, Jenny, described above and reported in Wilson (1999). Jenny received several months of rehabilitation, which could explain why she showed more recovery than Kertesz's patient. Zihl (2011) also mentions two prosopagnosic patients: one of Bruyer *et al.* (1983), who showed no recovery over a 12-month period, and one of Spillmann, Laskowski, Lange, Kasper, and Schmidt (2000), who had visual object agnosia, prosopagnosia and topographical agnosia. Although some recovery was seen over a three-year period, global perception remained severely impaired. The very interesting book by Goodale and Milner (2004) is the story of a patient who had very severe and widespread perceptual problems following carbon monoxide poisoning, including visual object agnosia and prosopagnosia. After 15 years she could function much better in her environment but she was, according to Goodale and Milner, compensating and using strategies to do this. The authors state that "Her damaged perceptual system has shown little recovery" (p. 125). Two cases reported in Wilson (1999) remained prosopagnosic for many years, with no sign of recovery.

In short, there is little to suggest that people with prosopagnosia will recover spontaneously.

Attempts to treat prosopagnosia

As with most treatment of people with brain injury, one can try to help people compensate for their difficulties or one can try to restore the damaged function. The patient described by Goodale and Milner learned to compensate very well for her widespread problems. She had a damaged ventral (the *what*) system but an intact dorsal (the *where*) system and was able to "use visuomotor tricks to compensate for the absence of form perception" (2004, p. 125). Many people with prosopagnosia learn to compensate by using voice, hairstyle, mannerisms and so forth. Richard (Wilson, 1999) had sustained two right hemisphere strokes in childhood and, as well as prosopagnosia, had numerous other visuo-perceptual and visuo-spatial problems. He could recognise people once they spoke, and compensatory strategies were employed for some of his other difficulties (e.g. he was unable to find his own mug from an array of eight mugs, so his mug was always placed alone on a different shelf). Some people with face blindness, including Claire, also lose the ability to recognise people's voices as well as their faces. In fact, she had lost a great deal of her knowledge about people, as we will see later in her account. This is consistent with the distinction made by Gainotti (2013) between prosopagnosia and a loss of semantic memory. Disrupted semantic knowledge for people is what Claire and her husband, Ed, feel is the major problem, rather than an inability to recognise faces.

As far as we know, there are no successful studies that have tried to restore or retrain face recognition skills in people with acquired prosopagnosia; the evidence for treatment of people with developmental prosopagnosia is limited, with no solid indication of generalisation to everyday life (see Table 2.1). Is it easier to help children with face blindness than adults? Apparently not, as Ellis and Young (1988), working with a child with acquired prosopagnosia, found little improvement in face recognition even after intense therapy comprising more than 1000 practice trials. Other studies have reported some experimental success at improving face recognition of photographs, but without evidence of generalisation to recognition of people in real life.

One of the most successful attempts at remediation was reported by Brunsdon, Coltheart, Nickels, and Joy (2006), who worked with AL, an eight-year-old boy with a severe perceptual impairment affecting both object and face processing. A comprehensive cognitive neuropsychological assessment indicated an impairment in encoding facial features. A "homework" training programme was designed to teach AL to encode internal facial features and recognise a set of 17 familiar face

Table 2.1 Summary of published attempts to treat prosopagnosia.

Authors	N	Disorder	Type of treatment	Improved face recognition?	Sustained post-treatment?	Generalisation to daily life?
Ellis and Young (1988)	1	AP	Facial discrimination (real faces)	No		
			Face matching	No		
			Facial discrimination (generated faces)	No		
			Face–name association	No		
De Haan et al. (1991)	1	AP	Semantic cuing	Limited	No	Unknown
Francis et al. (2002)	1	HSVE	Face–name learning and imagery	Yes	Unknown	No
			Semantic information and face learning	Yes	1 week	No
			Name and face learning	No		
			Learning of semantic information only	No		
Brunsdon et al. (2006)	1	Presumed developmental disorder	Facial feature analysis	Yes	3 months	Some anecdotal evidence
DeGutis et al. (2007)	1	Congenital disorder	Classifying facial features	Yes	No	Some anecdotal evidence

Study						
Powell et al. (2008)	20	ABI	Semantic association	Yes	Unknown	Unknown
Schmalzl et al. (2008)	1	Congenital disorder	Caricaturing	Yes	Unknown	Unknown
			Part recognition	Yes	Unknown	Unknown
			Facial feature analysis	Yes	1 month	Unknown
Dewar et al. (2009)	3	HSVE	Face, name and semantic information, with errorless learning	Yes	2 weeks	No
	1	SD		Yes	2 weeks	No
Bate et al. (under consideration)	1	HSVE	Facial discrimination	Yes	1 month	No

AP, acquired prosopagnosia; HSVE, Herpes simplex viral encephalitis; ABI, acquired brain injury; SD, semantic dementia.

photographs. On the back of each photograph was written the person's name, age, gender and three defining facial features (e.g. "big mouth"). In each training session, AL was shown each card, one at a time, and asked to identify the person. He was given the correct name if he misidentified the face, and he discussed the written clues with his parents. After 14 sessions AL had identified all of the faces with 100% accuracy on four consecutive sessions, and training was discontinued. Not only was the improvement in identifying the target photographs maintained at a three-month follow-up assessment, but also the training generalised to improve performance recognising different pictures of the same faces immediately after training. Furthermore, AL's performance on a feature discrimination task improved after treatment. Schmalzl, Palermo, Green, Brunsdon, and Coltheart (2008b) used the same training technique as Brunsdon and colleagues (2006) with K, a four-year-old girl with congenital prosopagnosia (Schmalzl et al., 2008a). After nine training sessions, she identified the faces with 100% accuracy, on four consecutive training sessions. K's identification of the trained faces was still flawless at a one-month follow-up. Analysis of her eye movements found that K directed more fixations to the internal features of both familiar and unfamiliar faces after training, indicating a generalised change in the way she viewed faces. What we do not know, however, is whether these two children were better able to recognise faces in everyday life.

In an intensive training programme, DeGutis and colleagues (2007) taught a woman (MZ) with congenital prosopagnosia to classify facial stimuli, which varied according to eyebrow and mouth height. Over two training sessions, MZ completed a staggering 8000 trials and continued to train at home. Afterwards, she performed normally on tasks of face perception and memory and functional MRI (fMRI) scans showed increased functional connectivity between several face-processing regions. However, during a period when training was suspended, MZ reported that the benefits of training faded and her improvement on psychophysiological measures of face perception was lost.

Looking at the treatment of people with acquired prosopagnosia, Zoltan (2007) offers some procedures to use to help people with face blindness, but she does not report any studies evaluating these methods. Powell, Letson, Davidoff, Valentine, and Greenwood (2008) investigated the rehabilitation of prosopagnosia among a broad pattern of cognitive impairments. Twenty patients each underwent three theory-driven training programmes to improve recognition of unfamiliar faces, semantic association (providing additional verbal information), caricaturing (providing caricatured versions of target faces), part recognition (focusing attention towards distinctive features) and a simple exposure procedure. In all groups, photographs of faces used during training and testing differed. Patients in all three targeted programmes were more accurate at identifying different photos of learned faces than a matched patient control group, who learned the same faces only under the simple exposure condition. Powell and colleagues (2008) found the three training programmes were of similar efficacy. Unfortunately, whether improvements generalised to unfamiliar faces or were maintained over time was not investigated.

Zihl (2011) mentions the work of Behrmann, Peterson, Moscovitch, and Suzuki (2006), who used practice as the treatment strategy with their patient. They found that object recognition improved but face recognition did not. In fact, it became worse! Controlled practice was also used with Jenny (who had associative visual object agnosia) and with Paula (who had apperceptive visual object agnosia), both of whom are reported in Wilson (1999). Neither of these patients, however, had severe problems with face recognition. Zihl (2011) also found practice worked for two patients with visual agnosia but it did not help their recognition of famous faces.

The patient with both prosopagnosia and severe amnesia described in Wilson (1999) was Martin, who had sustained a TBI. An attempt was made to teach him the names of the staff at the rehabilitation centre using a visual imagery method that had proved successful with other amnesic patients without prosopagnosia. Martin failed to reliably match any name to the correct face after 85 trials, at which point the treatment was abandoned. De Haan, Young, and Newcombe (1991) also had little success with PH, another TBI patient.

One carefully controlled treatment study was that of Francis, Riddoch, and Humphreys (2002). Their patient, NE, was a young woman who had survived HSVE (the same diagnosis as Claire). NE had prosopagnosia together with a person-based semantic memory disorder. Again, this is very similar to the problems faced by Claire. Treatment attempted to help NE learn to recognise new people and to recognise previously familiar people, with considerable success achieved in learning to recognise familiar faces. However, NE was still impaired in real life, although less impaired than either Ellis and Young's (1988) patient or De Haan and colleagues' patient. As Francis *et al.* (2002) suggest, "These results show a striking contrast between statistical significance in the laboratory and clinical significance in real life" (p. 24).

Bate *et al.* (under consideration) attempted to treat EM, a female adolescent who acquired prosopagnosia following encephalitis at the age of seven, with profound difficulties in perceiving and recognising faces. Analysis of her eye movements showed that she avoided looking at the internal features of the face, a pattern typical for people with prosopagnosia. EM used a practice-based online training programme for 14 weeks, which required her to discriminate between faces of increasing similarity. Following training, EM's ability to perceive faces improved and she spent more time looking at the inner features of the face. EM also improved in her recognition of personally known faces. However, she did not experience an improvement in her ability to recognise these faces in daily life and the training did not improve her performance on a test of learning and recognising new faces. One month after training, EM had maintained the improvement on the eye-tracking test, and to a lesser extent, her performance on the familiar faces test. Although these findings are encouraging evidence that, under some conditions, face perception skills can be improved, they are a further demonstration of how challenging it is to generalise from laboratory-based training to face recognition in daily life.

The final treatment study to be mentioned here is one in which Claire herself was included (Dewar, Patterson, Wilson, & Graham, 2009). She was one of four participants with semantic memory impairment for people (Claire was called VO in this paper). The questions to be answered were as follows: (1) could the four people learn new information; (2) did this generalise to new exemplars; and (3) was the learning maintained over time?

Following a multiple baseline assessment, ten faces of famous people (all well known to British subjects) were selected for training. The training consisted of providing a photograph plus a name plus a semantic fact. So, for example, a photograph of Tony Blair would be shown with his name written down together with the semantic fact "longest serving Labour Prime Minister". For each face a prominent feature was identified. Vanishing cues (VC) and expanded rehearsal were used to teach the name. In VC, one letter at a time was removed from names (e.g. Tony Blai_; Tony Bla_ _; Tony Bl_ _ _) and one word at a time for facts (e.g. Longest serving Prime _____; Longest serving _____ _____). The expanded rehearsal procedure continued as follows: once the name and fact were recalled correctly from the photograph alone, the photograph was removed for 10 seconds and then re-presented with the instructions "What is his/her name and what is he/she famous for?". If correct, the photograph was removed for 20, then 40, then 90 and then 180 seconds. If incorrect, a cue was given ("His initials are TB and he is a politician").

Two faces were trained at weekly sessions in addition to home practice. Recall of all faces was tested at the beginning of each session. Maintenance and generalisation of learning were also assessed. Like NE in the Francis *et al.* (2002) study, all four patients including VO (Claire) were able to correctly name the faces following training, but Claire needed cues to help her. Thus, she could learn some semantic information but not recognise the face itself without cues. There was evidence of generalisation of learning to different (profile) photographs of the ten people taught, although when the order of presentation was altered Claire's performance dropped a little.

In short, there is no good evidence that it is possible to retrain face recognition in people with prosopagnosia. Compensatory strategies should be encouraged and much can be done to help people and their families understand the problems. We can also provide rehabilitation to address the emotional and psychosocial difficulties and address problems with identity (Dewar & Gracey, 2007).

Before we continue with Claire's account, we are going to learn a little more about the theoretical aspects of prosopagnosia.

Chapter 3

Theoretical accounts of person recognition

How we understand face recognition

In the mid-1980s, at a time when neuropsychology was an established discipline with an already long history of investigation into language (McCarthy & Warrington, 1990), there had been very little research on how we recognise people. This began to change when a group of 25 mainly UK-based researchers started to meet annually to discuss face recognition. The result of this was captured in a model published by Bruce and Young (1986), which is still probably the most influential attempt to provide a theoretical framework of face recognition. Since its inception, research into face recognition has grown rapidly. This model is underpinned by three assumptions: (1) faces are unique in the way in which they are processed, (2) face processing involves several processes responsible for the production and storage of different kinds of information, and (3) faces are processed in successive stages. Recent evidence has led to further elaboration and revision of the model, which has come to be known as the Interactive Activation and Competition (IAC) model (Burton, 1998; Burton & Bruce, 1990, 1993; Burton, Bruce, & Hancock, 1999).

The Bruce and Young model

The Bruce and Young (1986) model suggests that, following early visual analysis, a stage common to other visual domains in which basic visual properties are encoded, we must produce a set of descriptions about a face. This is achieved in a stage called "structural encoding", where we create both view-centred descriptions and more abstract descriptions of the face's global configuration and local features. View-centred descriptions provide perceptual information for perceiving, analysing and categorising facial speech and facial expressions. Expression-independent descriptions are more abstract and provide information for the face recognition units (FRUs). Each FRU contains a viewpoint-invariant representation of a familiar face that is modality- and domain-specific. The activation of an FRU results in a feeling of familiarity for that face. This in turn accesses a person identity node (PIN), which is where the classification of a person occurs. As with the FRUs, there is one PIN for every known person. PINs are modality-free and store individually identifying semantic and biographical information. Once a PIN is activated by its corresponding FRU, a person's name becomes available.

In contrast to FRUs, which can only be activated by a face, PINs can be accessed via the face, name, voice or any other source of information that allows us to identify a person. The Bruce and Young (1986) model draws a distinction between the PINs, where person identification occurs, and the "cognitive system", which stores associative and episodic information about a person, such as when we saw them last. Bruce and Young (1986) also distinguish between the more passive familiar face recognition and the more active analysis and encoding of unfamiliar faces; the latter is termed "directed visual processing", a separate component to the cognitive system.

The IAC model

The IAC model (Burton, 1998; Burton & Bruce, 1990, 1993; Burton et al., 1999) is the most recent revision of the Bruce and Young (1986) model. The IAC model differs from its predecessor in several respects. As in the Bruce and Young (1986) model, it suggests that information from different modalities converges in the PINs. However, to account for cross-domain priming between faces and names (Young, Hellawell, & De Haan, 1988), the IAC model suggests that familiarity decisions occur in the PINs. The other important difference is that, whereas in the Bruce and Young (1986) model the PINs store semantic information, in the IAC model PINs do not store this information, but provide a modality-free gateway to a single amodal semantic system about known individuals, comprising semantic information units (SIUs). SIUs can be shared between individuals. For example, an SIU containing semantic information 'royals', would be activated if the PIN for either Prince William or Kate Middleton became active. Information about a person is coded in the form of a link between the PIN and SIUs. The IAC model makes explicit that the PINs can be accessed by other modalities, such as names (name recognition units, NRUs) or voices (voice recognition units).

In the IAC model, the FRUs, PINs, SIUs, NRUs and lexical output engage in interactive activation and competition (McClelland, 1981), a simple connectionist architecture. The connections within each pool of units (e.g. the SIUs) are inhibitory, whereas between pools they are excitatory. Activation passes between units along connections. Initially all connections are bidirectional and of equal strength. Activation is driven towards a standard resting state by global decay. Face identification occurs with activation between a FRU, PIN, SIU and NRU.

At first glance, the assumptions made by the Bruce and Young (1986) and IAC models seem straightforward, and their differences may appear trivial. However, simple assumptions can have far-reaching implications for how we understand the way in which the brain processes information, and these apparently small differences have questioned our fundamental understanding of how and where the brain stores information about people. As we shall discuss, neuropsychology is well placed to provide insight into the brain's structure and processes, and patients such as Claire, with their unique challenges, can tell us a great deal.

Claire is unique, both in terms of her particular challenges and her remarkable insight. Because of this, Claire's time is much in demand and she has collaborated with a number of researchers. As a result, there was a relatively good amount of data on her person-based knowledge by the time I (Joe Mole) first met her. This is just as well, as Claire's difficulty recognising people appears to be much deeper than prosopagnosia. In order to help us understand Claire's challenges in more detail, we assessed her using standardised neuropsychological tests and tests of object- and person-based knowledge (see Table 3.1). Where we could not compare Claire's performance to published normative data, we compared it to the performance of a group of four women with acquired brain injury, who were from a similar socio-economic background and of a similar age. Comparisons were made using the computer programme SINGLIMS (Crawford & Garthwaite, 2002), which is designed to compare an individual case to a small control group. We now discuss our efforts to understand Claire's difficulties with knowing people, structured around three questions of theoretical interest.

1. *Is Claire's difficulty recognising people associated with perception or memory? Is Claire a case of apperceptive or associative prosopagnosia?*

The Bruce and Young model (1986) makes the assumption that faces are processed in successive stages, implying that damage can occur at any stage in the model and, because several processes proceed hierarchically, impairment at one stage will impede processing at a later stage. In support of this idea is the distinction made by Lissauer (1890) between

Table 3.1 Claire's performance on standardised neuropsychological tests and people and landmark knowledge tasks.

	2004	2005	2013
Perception			
Benton Facial Recognition Test	42/54	46/54	39/54
VOSP			
Position discrimination	20/20		
Number location	10/10		
Memory			
Graded Places Test			**4/30**
Graded Places Test, Description from Name			**16/60**
Famous Face Familiarity Task			**20/75**
Famous Name Familiarity Task			74/75
Social Cognition			
Emotion Recognition Task: Ekman & Friesen faces			
Happiness		**9/10**	**9/10**
Surprise		**5/10**	7/10
Fear		**5/10**	**4/10**
Sadness		7/10	7/10
Disgust		**6/10**	9/10
Anger		7/10	6/10
TASIT Part A: Emotion Evaluation Test			
Happy			4/4
Surprised			4/4
Neutral			**0/4**
Sad			2/4
Angry			3/4
Anxious			3/4
Revolted			**3/4**

Bold indicates impaired performance relative to published norms or a matched control group, calculated using SINGLIMS non-parametric statistics. VOSP, Visual Object and Space Perception Battery (Warrington & James, 1991); TASIT, The Awareness of Social Inference Test (McDonald et al., 2003).

two types of recognition disorders, or "agnosias". A deficit could arise from an inability to perceive stimuli, an "apperceptive agnosia", or an impairment ascribing meaning to what is perceived, an "associative agnosia". Extending this, De Renzi and colleagues (De Renzi, 1986b; De Renzi et al., 1991) have argued that difficulty recognising faces can result from "apperceptive prosopagnosia", the inability to form an accurate percept, or "associative prosopagnosia", the loss of visual memories of previously learned faces or inability to access these memories. In terms of the Bruce and Young (1986) model (Figure 3.1), apperceptive prosopagnosia would be caused by impairment at the level of structural encoding, whereas associative prosopagnosia would result from either disconnection between perceptual encoding and FRUs or damage to the FRUs. By contrast, associative prosopagnosia might be explained by the IAC model as damage to the FRUs or by disconnection between the FRUs and PINs. Anatomically, face processing is supported by a number of distributed brain regions, which, consistent with the assumptions of the Bruce and Young (1986) model, appear to form a hierarchical network (Haxby, Hoffman, & Gobbini, 2000; Zhen, Fang, & Liu, 2013). Usually, apperceptive prosopagnosia is caused by lesions of the posterior part of this network, including areas such as the inferior occipital

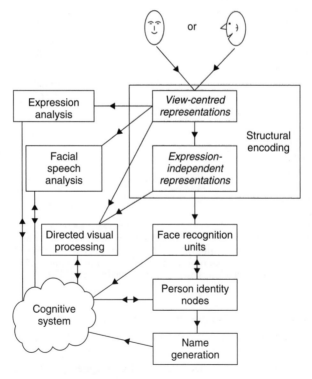

Figure 3.1 The Bruce and Young (1986) model.

gyrus (occipital face area, OFA) and the lateral fusiform gyrus (fusiform face area, FFA), whereas associative forms are mainly due to lesions of the right anterior temporal lobe (ATL) (Gainotti, 2013). However, Farah (1990) has challenged the distinction between apperceptive and associative prosopagnosia, arguing that associative visual agnosia may actually be caused by a perceptual impairment. According to Farah, such patients may appear to perform normally on tasks of object perception, but may take an abnormally long time to do so.

Claire

In terms of the Bruce and Young model, Claire has no difficulty with early visual analysis, as Claire performs normally on the Visual Object and Space Perception Battery (Warrington & James, 1991), a test of perceiving basic visual properties of stimuli (see Table 3.1). Indeed, when shown 'Mooney faces', faces with luminance values transformed to black or white to degrade facial features (Kanwisher, Tong, & Nakayama, 1998; Mondloch, Pathman, Le Grand, & Maurer, 2003), Claire is able to detect that a face is present.

Claire's ability to perceive faces at the level of structural encoding appears to be relatively normal. When assessed with the Benton Facial Recognition Test (Benton & Van Allen, 1968), her performance is consistently unimpaired and not unusually slow (see Table 3.1). However, it should be noted that, on the most recent testing session, her performance was within the borderline range. As this test requires matching of faces across different viewpoints and lighting conditions, it appears that Claire can create both view-centred and expression-independent descriptions, at the level of structural encoding. Thus, we would argue that Claire's difficulty with faces is unlikely to be apperceptive in nature.

Claire's ability to recognise emotional expressions was assessed using the Emotion Recognition Task: Ekman & Friesen faces (Ekman & Friesen, 1976). When tested formally, Claire previously had difficulty with several emotional expressions, but now only has trouble recognising happiness and fear (see Table 3.1). Although Claire correctly identified the expression of many of the faces showing happiness, her performance was still poorer than the normative control group, as this expression is particularly easy to identify. As the Bruce and Young model predicts that the basic structural encoding of a face provides information for the processing of facial identity and expression, performance on tests of emotion recognition are often used as a measure of face perception abilities (Blonder, Bowers, & Heilman, 1991). However, impairments in recognising facial expressions can occur for other reasons (Calder & Young, 2005). For example, damage to the amygdala can result in a disproportionate impairment in detecting fear over other emotions, which may not reflect a difficulty interpreting emotion from faces per se, but a more general problem processing fear from several sensory inputs (Calder, Lawrence, & Young, 2001). On The Awareness of Social Inference Test (McDonald, Flanagan, Rollins, & Kinch, 2003), a test of interpreting the emotions portrayed by actors in short video clips, with both facial and vocal clues, Claire showed difficulty with several emotions. Thus, it seems that Claire has a general difficulty with emotional interpretation, which is not restricted to face processing.

2. *Does Claire only have difficulty recognising people from their faces? Is it best to conceive of her difficulties as associative prosopagnosia or as a multi-modal recognition disorder?*

Familiarity of faces and names

Associative prosopagnosia is thought to result from damage to the right ATL. However, it has frequently been argued that people with damage to this area also have difficulty in recognising people from other modalities, such as their name or voice (Gainotti, 2013). In his early paper, in which he discusses nine cases of associative prosopagnosia, De Renzi (1986b) did not investigate the possibility that these individuals were impaired at recognising people through other modalities.

The Bruce and Young (1986) model assumes that familiarity feelings occur in modality-specific recognition units. According to Gainotti (2007), this view is consistent with more recent models of person recognition that assume a continuity between the way in which we process perceptual and conceptual information (Gainotti, Barbier, & Marra, 2003; Snowden, Thompson, & Neary, 2004). In support of this, patients with right ATL atrophy often have a loss of familiarity and person-specific information from faces, and patients with left ATL atrophy are frequently impaired at recognising famous names (Gainotti, 2007). Furthermore, impairments in recognising familiar faces, despite nearly normal face perception, and in the ability to retrieve semantic information from names, have also been described in patients with analogous right ATL damage with different aetiologies (Pancaroglu *et al.*, 2011). In contrast to the Bruce and Young model, the IAC model assumes that feelings of familiarity occur in the PINs, where information from different modalities converges. Thus, the Bruce and Young and IAC models could make different predictions about whether familiarity feelings generated by the face and name of the same person should converge or dissociate. The Bruce and Young model's assumption, of a modality-specific locus of familiarity judgement, would predict the independence of familiarity feelings from a person's face and name, whereas the IAC's assumption of a supra-modal locus of familiarity decision would predict a co-occurrence (see Figure 3.2).

Claire

To investigate Claire's ability to judge people as familiar, we showed her famous faces and names, which were created and very kindly provided

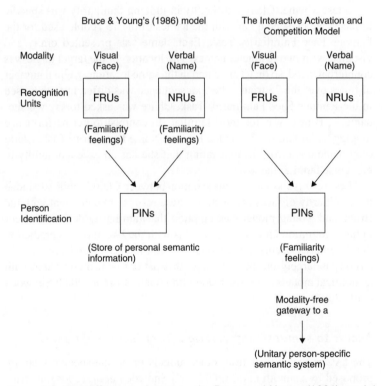

Figure 3.2 Key differences between the Bruce and Young (1986) model and the Interactive Activation and Competition Model (Burton, 1998; Burton & Bruce, 1990, 1993; Burton et al., 1999). FRU, face recognition unit; NRU, name recognition unit; PIN, person identity node. (Adapted from Gainotti, 2007.)

by Professor McCarthy and her team. In the Famous Face Familiarity Task, 75 greyscale faces were presented of people who were prominent and highly recognisable figures from 1985–2013. Each face was presented with two visually similar distracter faces, and the location of the target was counterbalanced, so that it appeared in the same location an equal number of times over the 75 trials. Claire was asked to say whether face A, B or C was most familiar to her and to name it if she could. Claire's accuracy in picking out the most famous face was at chance and significantly poorer than that of the control group (see Table 3.1). Claire's difficulty in judging facial familiarity is so great that, when we have tested her in the past, she is unable to recognise her own face as familiar. Claire is certainly living with one of the most profound face recognition difficulties that we have encountered.

To test whether Claire's difficulty in judging familiarity was specific to faces, we presented her with the names of the 75 people used for the Famous Face Familiarity Task. Each name was presented orally and visually, with two distracter names. The location of the target name was counterbalanced, so that it appeared in the same location an equal number of times over the 75 trials. The trial sequence was different to that used in the Famous Face Familiarity Task. Claire was asked to say whether name A, B or C was the most familiar. In contrast to her performance judging facial familiarity, on the Famous Name Familiarity Task, Claire only made one error, demonstrating that she has an excellent ability to recognise familiar names.

These results show a clear dissociation between Claire's ability to judge the familiarity of faces and names. These results are consistent with the Bruce and Young model's assumption that familiarity decisions occur in the recognition units and are at odds with the IAC model's prediction that familiarity occurs in the modality-free PINs. Because Claire's ATL atrophy is largely on the right side, this pattern is also consistent with anatomical models of person recognition (Gainotti *et al.*, 2003; Snowden *et al.*, 2004).

Access to semantic information from faces and names

The IAC model differs from other models of person-specific memory proposed by Gainotti *et al.* (2003) and Snowden *et al.* (2004) in terms of how person-based semantic knowledge is thought to be organised. Several authors have argued that person-specific knowledge can be seen as a network, in which the right and left temporal lobes process and store different components of the semantic system (Gainotti *et al.*, 2003;

Snowden *et al.*, 2004). In the left hemisphere, where cognition is mainly shaped and modulated by language, semantic knowledge of people could be stored in a verbal format (Balaban & Waxman, 1997), whereas in the right hemisphere, where faces and voices are typically processed, semantic information could be stored in a perceptual format (Coslett & Saffran, 1989, 1992; Gainotti, 2004, 2006). Thus, person-specific knowledge is distributed and not all represented in the same format or in the same place. According to this perspective, modality-specific perceptual information is actually part of semantic knowledge and not just a means of accessing it (Snowden *et al.*, 2004). This perspective is also similar to more general models of semantic memory that suggest semantic knowledge is represented in the same sensory-motor format in which it has been constructed (Allport, 1985; Gallese & Lakoff, 2005; Warrington & Shallice, 1979). In support of this view is evidence of a double dissociation between patients with poor comprehension for words relative to pictures (McCarthy & Warrington, 1988) and impaired visual semantics with intact verbal comprehension (McCarthy & Warrington, 1986).

In contrast to these models, the IAC model assumes that person-specific semantic information is held in a single amodal abstract store. This is thought to represent abstract information, so information from all modalities is stored in the same place. This store can be accessed via the PINs, which are also not specific to any one modality. Perceptual information such as a name or a face do not form part of the semantic store, but are merely a means of accessing it. This standpoint is consistent with general models of semantic memory (Pylyshyn, 1973; Fodor, 1975, 1987; Humphreys & Riddoch, 1988; Caramazza, Hillis, Rapp, & Romani, 1990; Lambon Ralph, Graham, Patterson, & Hodges, 1999), which suggest a clear distinction between modality-specific input/output mechanisms and a single abstract semantic system. Consistent with this view is the finding that, in patients with ATL atrophy, the ability to give a core definition of a specific word can be highly predictive of the ability to comprehend and name pictures (Lambon Ralph *et al.*, 1999).

The IAC model and models proposed by Gainotti *et al.* (2003) and Snowden *et al.* (2004) make very different predictions about how person-based semantic memory is organised. The IAC model would predict, assuming that familiarity for an item is intact, that a similar amount of semantic information can be retrieved in response to face and name cues. In contrast, models proposed by Gainotti *et al.* (2003) and Snowden *et al.* (2004) would assume that an impairment in accessing semantic information from a face can be dissociated from an impairment accessing semantic information from a name.

Claire

In previous work with Claire, Dewar, Patterson, Wilson, and Graham (2009) conducted a comprehensive neuropsychological assessment, finding that Claire had great difficulty in recalling names and semantic facts from people's faces. Claire was also found to have difficulty making judgements about whether names of famous people were semantically associated. These findings are consistent with Claire's account (Part II) of her loss of some person-based semantic memory and/or challenges accessing semantic information from names and faces. Theoretically, her performance seems to lend support to the predictions made by the IAC model. However, the alternative models proposed by Gainotti *et al.* (2003) and Snowden *et al.* (2004) are also plausible, as her difficulties with perceptual and verbal person-based knowledge could be associated with extensive right ATL atrophy and more limited left ATL atrophy, respectively.

3. *Is it only people that Claire has difficulty recognising? Does Claire have a category specific recognition disorder?*

As discussed, some theorists propose that the brain processes and stores different types of semantic information differently. For example, knowledge about natural things (e.g. animals or fruit) and knowledge about artefacts (e.g. tools, household objects) may be processed by distinct neural mechanisms (Caramazza & Shelton, 1998). There is also evidence to suggest that information about people may be stored in a further semantic subsystem. However, it is debated whether this system is specific for people, or for any instances of "unique entities".

Damasio and colleagues (Damasio, 1989, 1990; Damasio, Damasio, Tranel, & Brandt, 1991) have argued that the rostral regions of the temporal lobes could be "convergence zones", which bind together distributed conceptual representations. Importantly, this mechanism may process "unique entities" (such as people or landmarks). The same authors (Damasio, Grabowski, Tranel, Hichwa, & Damasio, 1996; Tranel, Damasio, & Damasio, 1997; Damasio, Tranel, Grabowski, Adolphs, & Damasio, 2004; Grabowski *et al.*, 2001, 2003; Tranel, 2006) have elaborated this hypothesis, predicting that the left temporal polar region is associated with the retrieval of words signifying "unique entities", whereas the right temporal polar regions may be associated with the retrieval of conceptual knowledge about the same entities. Thus, this more recent account is consistent with a non-unitary account of semantic representation. In support of this hypothesis is evidence

from people with a particular form of fronto-temporal lobe degeneration, referred to as "semantic dementia". In cases of semantic dementia
mainly affecting the right side, a person-based recognition deficit is
often associated with more extensive loss of semantic knowledge, such
as for famous events (Barbarotto, Capitani, Spinnler, & Trivelli, 1995;
Kitchener & Hodges, 1999; Joubert et al., 2003), food (Gorno Tempini
et al., 2004) or famous places (Barbarotto et al., 1995; Gentileschi,
Sperber, & Spinnler, 1999; Joubert et al., 2004; Gainotti, Ferraccioli,
Quaranta, & Marra, 2008).

In contrast to this perspective, the IAC model predicts that processing
of person-specific information is separable from that of general semantic knowledge. Evidence in support of this has come from patients with
profound, and apparently selective, deficits for proper nouns (Carney &
Temple, 1993). However, more recent studies have shown that many of
these patients show deficits that extend to other classes of proper noun,
such as geographical names (Hanley & Kay, 1998). Particularly strong
evidence has been reported of a double dissociation on the same battery
of tests between a patient with left lateralised temporal lobe atrophy, who
demonstrated an impairment in object and animal knowledge in the context of relatively preserved knowledge of famous people, and a patient
with focal right temporal lobe atrophy, who showed a severe impairment
in person-specific semantics in the context of a mild deficit on general
semantic memory tasks (Thompson et al., 2004). Unfortunately, the only
unique entities used in this study were person-based, so these results could
support the existence of a semantic system specifically for people or a system responsible for knowledge of unique entities. However, an important
case has been reported by Evans, Heggs, Antoun, and Hodges (1995) of
a patient with right ATL atrophy, who was impaired at recognising faces
yet was able to identify unique exemplars from other categories, such as
buildings and flowers. In addition, a case has been reported by Gainotti
et al. (2003) of a patient with a specific deficit in recognising people.
Both these cases support the IAC's assumption of a specific person-
based semantic system.

Claire

To investigate whether Claire's difficulty with person-based semantics is
selective for people or extends to unique entities, we asked her to name
a series of famous landmarks, in a test developed by McCarthy, Evans,
and Hodges (1996). Several weeks later, we also presented Claire with
the names of these landmarks and asked her to give a verbal description

of each item. The responses of Claire and her control group were rated by two independent markers, who followed the same guidelines for scoring the accuracy of each response on a scale of 0 to 2. On both tasks Claire had great difficulty (see Table 3.1).

We observed that the landmarks that Claire was able to visually recognise and describe well were located either in the UK or France. To investigate this further, we asked Claire to draw a map of the world with no guidance. As can be seen in Figure 3.3, Claire showed relatively good knowledge of the UK and its surrounding countries, but had more difficulty as she began to sketch the rest of the world. As noted by Mondini and Semenza (2006), the study of spared knowledge can be informative and may lead to potentially revealing patterns. Frequently, people with ATL atrophy have more difficulty with some faces than others. For example, knowledge can be preserved for faces that have autobiographical significance (Gainotti *et al.*, 2003) or may have taken on iconic status, such as that of Silvio Berlusconi (Mondini & Semenza, 2006). People with this condition are also found to be consistently better at identifying the names of places of which they have had some personal experience (Snowden, Griffiths, & Neary, 1994).

Thus, it appears that Claire has difficulty with both person-based semantic information and knowledge of unique entities. As it is not clear whether Claire's difficulties reflect a disruption to two separate semantic systems, one for people and one for unique entities, or simply to one store for unique entities, we are unable to draw any firm theoretical conclusions regarding the specificity of person-based semantics.

Figure 3.3 World map, drawn by Claire in 2014.

Summary

Claire does not appear to have problems perceiving faces. Nevertheless, she has a profound impairment in judging facial familiarity. Although she is able to judge familiarity from names, we cannot assume that her inability to judge familiarity is specific to faces. Anecdotal evidence suggests that she can judge some voices as familiar, but future research will be necessary to establish the extent of this ability. Claire has great difficulty with semantic information about people, which she cannot access from names or faces, but this is not specific to people, as she also has trouble with semantic memory of famous landmarks, which are also unique entities. The more we learn about Claire the more we admire her resourcefulness in the face of rare and testing challenges.

Chapter 4

The self and identity

What do we mean by "self" and "identity"?

Self is the essential nature of a person that endures over time (Brinthaupt & Lipka, 1992), while identity refers to perceptions of the unique and persisting qualities that distinguish self from others (Dumont, 2013). If we look at the history of this topic, we see that people have been interested in what makes us who we are, what defines us and how we make sense of our lives, for a great many years. In Ancient Greece, Aristotle recognised the importance of self-knowledge and how our relationships with others help us to form our sense of self. Furthermore, he acknowledged the importance of occupation to achieve personal development and reach one's potential through participation (cited by Ownsworth, 2014).

Over a century ago, William James (1890) said that the self is what a person calls "me" and that one of the major requirements for the persistence of "self" is the continuum of recollections (Ben-Yishay, 2008). James distinguished between the subjective self, the "I" and the objective self, the "Me". He said the Material Me comprised the body and possessions, the Social Me was oneself as perceived by one's peers, and the Spiritual Me involved one's inner or subjective being. He felt that self-esteem "depends entirely on what we back ourselves to be and do" (p. 310).

This echoes the writings of John Locke (1632–1704), who conceived of personal identity as a matter of psychological continuity (Locke & Winkler, 1996). He argued that, although the brain and body may change, consciousness remains the same. It is our memory that gives us identity. More recently, Baddeley and Wilson (1986), looking at the autobiographical memory of people with amnesia, found that those who had lost many of their autobiographical memories were anxious or agitated, causing difficulty for the rehabilitation team. They recognised the importance of autobiographical memory for the idea of self, saying "it is hard not to wonder to what extent having access to one's previous life is an important part of one's concept of one's self as a person" (p. 250). Since then, many others have addressed the issue of autobiographical memory and the concept of self. For example, Wilson and Ross (2003) stated "We are what we remember" (p. 137), while Williams, Conway, and Cohen (2008) suggested that autobiographical memory performs a self-representative function by using personal memories to create and maintain a coherent self-identity over time. Douglas (2013) says that our concept of self helps us make sense of our lives. She goes on to say that self-concept can be viewed as a multi-dimensional, internal representation of the individual.

A special issue of the journal *Neuropsychological Rehabilitation* addressed the topic of "The self and identity in rehabilitation" (Gracey & Ownsworth, 2008). In this issue, Naylor and Clare (2008) recognised that sense of self is threatened by a combination of poor autobiographical memory and awareness of this problem.

The self comprises the collective characteristics we think of as our own, including bodily and internal psychological states. These are both consistent characteristics and characteristics continually under construction. The sense of self reflects our past and present selves as well as our possible selves, or who we might become (Markus & Nurius, 1986). Self-identity refers to awareness of one's inner sameness and continuity, yet is continually under construction (Ownsworth, 2014). To return to Locke (Locke & Winkler, 1996) we see that he believed that the sense of self requires consciousness of one's past and future thoughts and actions, as well as awareness of these processes in the present moment.

Current views of self and identity

There is a multitude of theories and models addressing the self and identity, which are comprehensively and excellently addressed by Ownsworth (2014). Some, but not all, of the major ones are addressed here. Social identity theory (Tajfel & Turner, 1979) refers to a person's self-concept derived from his or her perceived membership of a relevant social group. According to this theory and to the theory of self-categorisation (Jetten *et al.*, 2012), group memberships are integral to our sense of self and are not easily separable. For example, when people are forced to give up work they lose their professional identity and may suffer loss of self-esteem.

Loss of group membership may mean less social support, poorer quality of life and an impaired sense of well-being. Haslam *et al.* (2008) applied social identity theory to survivors of stroke. They suggested that membership of multiple groups buffered people against the negative effects of brain injury. To determine if this was the case, they looked at the membership of multiple groups prior to stroke and found that continuity of social identity (maintenance of group membership after stroke) predicted well-being. Others, such as Freeman (1992), envisage the self as an ongoing narrative or, in other words, "Simply stated, on some level, we are the stories we tell about ourselves" (p. 25).

Why brain damage can lead to problems with the self and identity

A new book has recently been published addressing the topic of self and identity after brain injury (Ownsworth, 2014). Ownsworth says an injury to the brain can affect virtually any aspect of functioning and, at the deepest level, can alter one's sense of self or the essential qualities that define who we are. As one of the Oliver Zangwill clients said, "I live in the ruins of my old self". Figure 4.1 is an illustration of how different people's self-representation can be after brain injury (Ownsworth, 2013).

Ownsworth (2014) lists several reasons why a neurological insult can cause problems with one's sense of self and self-identity. First, the neural networks that support one's sense of self can be disturbed by a

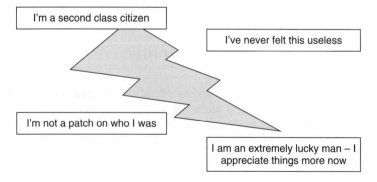

■ How is sense of self affected by brain injury?

I'm a second class citizen

I've never felt this useless

I'm not a patch on who I was

I am an extremely lucky man – I appreciate things more now

Figure 4.1 People's self-representations after brain injury may differ (Ownsworth, 2013).

brain problem (Feinberg, 2011). Second, changes in one's sense of self and personal identity are known to occur after stressful life events such as bereavement or divorce (Orth, Trzesniewski, & Robins, 2010); these changes may be positive or negative. Third, situations may occur that can lead to discrepancies between one's idea of who we once were and who we are now (as happened with Claire, who developed severe prosopagnosia and loss of knowledge about people, leading to a lack of what she felt to be the essence of her former self). Fourth, views on one's self can be altered as a result of therapeutic interventions. Indeed, rehabilitation for survivors of brain injury frequently involves attempts to persuade people to accept themselves as they are now.

Levack, Kayes, and Fadyl (2010) carried out a meta-analysis to determine the experience of traumatic brain injury (TBI). Twenty-three studies were included and eight inter-related themes identified: (1) mind/body disconnect; (2) disconnect with pre-injury identity; (3) social disconnect; (4) emotional sequelae; (5) internal and external resources; (6) reconstruction of self-identity; (7) reconstruction of a place in the world; and (8) reconstruction of personhood.

Another influential model from recent years is the "Y" shaped model (Gracey, Evans, & Malley, 2009).The authors believe that "A complex and dynamic set of biological, psychological and social factors interact to determine the consequences of acquired brain injury" (p. 867). Their model integrates findings from psychosocial adjustment, awareness and well-being. It is, essentially, an attempt to reduce the discrepancy between the old "me" and the new "me". This is a crucial part of the Oliver Zangwill Centre (OZC) programme. As we see later in this chapter, Fergus Gracey, who was Claire's principal psychologist when she was at the OZC, describes some of the joint work they did together as part of Claire's rehabilitation.

Douglas (2013) carried out a qualitative investigation to gain insight into how adults who had survived a severe or very severe TBI understood themselves several years after injury. The hope was that this would describe processes to help rehabilitation. From the patients' narratives, a dynamic and multifaceted model of self was derived (see Figure 4.2).

Ownsworth (2014), one of the leading experts on self and identity issues after brain injury, discusses the links between task failure, self-discrepancy, threat appraisal, avoidance and negative self-concept, which seems to fit Claire and her views of herself and her situation very well, as we see below. Figure 4.3 presents Ownsworth's (2014) model illustrating these links.

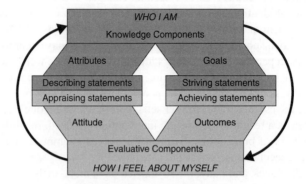

Figure 4.2 Douglas's (2013) model of "Conceptualising self after trau-matic brain injury" (Douglas, 2013, reproduced with permis-sion of Informa Healthcare).

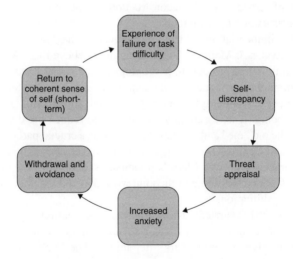

Figure 4.3 Cycle of appraisals, anxiety and avoidance, and the impact on self-concept (Ownsworth, 2014, p. 64, fig. 4.3, reprinted with permission of Psychology Press).

Claire and her loss of self and identity

Continuity and stability of self are helpful for individuals to accept that the world and their own actions are predictable (Ownsworth, 2014). It is this loss of continuity that seems to have affected Claire; she has lost many of her memories and feels she is no longer the person she once was. Yet she is not severely amnesic. She is not, for example, like CW (Wilson *et al.*, 2008), who forgets after a few seconds everything that has gone on before. Indeed, in her neuropsychological assessments carried out in 2004 and 2005, Claire's verbal memory was a relative strength. However, in addition to a very severe prosopagnosia she has lost knowledge of people and also appears to have a fairly lengthy retrograde amnesia, both of which seem to have a big impact on sense of self and loss of identity. This has implications for rehabilitation and confirms the increasing recognition that it is essential to address identity change issues after brain injury. Nochi (1997) found that loss of sense of self after injury was accompanied by a reduction in the individual's social activity. This is probably true, in part, for Claire, but, in many ways she seems to have an active social life, particularly for someone with such severe problems. Others have found that as the discrepancy between ratings of past self and current self increase, so does emotional dysfunction (Wright & Telford, 1996; Cantor *et al.*, 2005). This seems true of Claire, she feels a very different person to her pre-injury self and is therefore highly anxious and self-critical. Cooper-Evans, Alderman, Knight, and Oddy (2008) reported that people with more severe global deficits had higher self-esteem, which may have been mediated by poorer self-awareness. In contrast, Claire's cognitive deficits are severe but selective, which means that she has a good awareness of how fundamentally different she is from her past self, which elicits high levels of emotional distress.

All of the models described above would appear to be relevant to Claire's difficulties. Social Identity Theory and Self-Categorisation Theory can explain why Claire's loss of her professional role has had such an impact on her self-esteem. In Freeman's narrative view, Claire's life story has been disrupted and she finds it difficult to connect her story. Many of the eight themes identified in Levack *et al.*'s (2010) meta-analysis apply to Claire: she certainly has a disconnection with her pre-injury identity. There is a social disconnect because she does not know her former family and friends. The emotional consequences are obvious: Claire is highly anxious but she has both internal and external resources. Internally, she is a fighter—she does not give up and strives to make sense of her changed circumstances. Her external resources include a supportive husband and social network. She is constantly trying to reconstruct herself and fluctuates between saying "I can't be a good friend/mother/wife because I don't remember information about people" to saying "This is me now, I have to accept it". This development is also described in Levack *et al.*'s seventh and eighth constructs (reconstruction of a place in the world and reconstruction of personhood). Gracey *et al.*'s (2009) "Y" shaped model applies to Claire perfectly in that it refers to attempts to reduce the discrepancy between the "old and the new me", something Claire is always trying to accommodate. This way of understanding self and identity issues appears to be somewhat similar to Douglas' (2013) model, which attempts to reconcile the discrepancy between *knowledge* of one's self and *evaluation* of one's self. Ownsworth's (2014) model offers, perhaps the best explanation of Claire's circumstances; she is certainly negative about herself (the central node), which increases her anxiety, and she withdraws from situations because she does not know who anybody is. She tried to return to her former self when she first went home from hospital but could not, thereby experiencing failure. This increased her self-discrepancy and sense of threat, which, in turn, increased her anxiety, and so the circle continued.

However, some people with identity and self issues can benefit from rehabilitation and change how they view themselves. Ownsworth (2014) suggests that such people can develop a stronger sense of who they are and what they stand for—they can change from saying "I have never been this useless" to saying "I've come to appreciate what else matters" and from saying "I'm still a second class citizen" to saying "I now say what's on my mind". Dan, one of Ownsworth's patients, said "Everything I do through each day is a personal challenge. I try to think positively but at the same time I expect nothing; my idea being that high expectations sometimes carry great disappointments. I have a need to be accepted, but life has taught me that if people can't accept me for who I am, then that's their problem and not mine. I must be true to myself and do the best that I can within my limitations" (Ownsworth, 2014).

One of Claire's favourite pieces of equipment to help her remember is SenseCam, a small camera usually worn around the neck that takes pictures automatically (see Figure 4.4). It does not have a viewfinder but is fitted with a wide-angle (fish-eye) lens that maximizes its field-of-view. This means that nearly everything in the wearer's view is captured by the camera (Hodges, Berry, & Wood 2011). Originally designed by Microsoft, SenseCam was, until recently, marketed by Vicon revue (www.viconrevue.com). Vicon Revue has now ceased marketing, and at the time of writing the camera is now marketed as "Autographer" (www.autographer.com). This device passively records experiences, without conscious thought. It allows full participation in the event being photo-graphed and is plugged into a standard personal computer so the images can be viewed individually or as a jerky "movie". Claire spends a consid-erable amount of time viewing her images.

Figure 4.4 Claire using SenseCam to film the OZC therapy dog.

During her stay at the OZC, Claire's psychological therapy was carried out by Fergus Gracey, the lead clinical psychologist at the time, and Bonnie-Kate Dewar continued to be involved. In November 2013, I interviewed Fergus to ask what he remembered of his sessions with Claire. This is a transcript of the interview:

> Claire was very motivated and wanted to learn. She engaged well with the rehabilitation process at the OZC and was happy using strategies to manage her memory and other difficulties, which she did well—although she was still anxious about them.
> As we came to the end of rehabilitation where many people would start feeling positive and hopeful about the future (they would look

back on recent situations and see they were managing better), Claire had difficulty with this. This was despite reports from Ed and other people that she was doing well. Claire, however, was coming back saying it was terrible and she was embarrassing herself. Being aware of her difficulties with memory and the potential for SenseCam (work was just starting to be carried out then) to help with that, we wondered if using SenseCam might help Claire review a situation in a more intensive detailed way. It might be a way of not only updating information about the situation but help her with her *feeling* of who she was.

What we actually did with her was work with her and her husband to try to collect information in a more traditional CBT way, to try to collect information using a diary and a log book—a "positive experiences log". To try to capture positive examples and for Claire to be reminded of these as often and as practical and appropriate. We didn't actually get so far as to target those negatively biased memories with a specific SenseCam intervention. That is something we hoped to do, as Claire uses SenseCam a lot, but we haven't done that targeting.

Working with Claire has made me think about my interest in identity change. She has made me think about the cognitive and neuropsychological processes that might be required to enable that. I don't know if Claire is someone who has a particular view of herself which tends to be negatively biased and that's an enduring trait of her personality and that's what we're dealing with or if it's a neuropsychological issue. My feeling is it's the latter. She is otherwise positive, she engaged in rehabilitation. Often people who have low self-esteem are more avoidant of rehabilitation and have more issues with engagement. She learned strategy use and engaged fully but she retained an enduring negative sense of her own identity despite evidence to the contrary from others. This formed part of the chapter with Tamara (Ownsworth & Gracey, 2008) where one of the things we looked at was how autobiographical memory and executive function systems play a part in the change process. For some, either the encoding of experiences or the use of drawing on experiences to have a sense of oneself could be impaired as a result of a particular kind of brain injury. This is a hypothesis yet to be tested.

Claire's illness has affected the cognitive processes that seem to be so important in forming a sense of personal and social identity. The selective nature of her deficits means that Claire has a good insight into her problems, which is all the more distressing for her. Nevertheless, Claire is finding a place. She is a mother, a friend, a wife, a writer, a speaker, a collaborator, as well as a good person. Although she does not always accept the changes to her sense of self, she may be slowly coming to accept that this new Claire is someone she can live with

Part II

Chapter 5

Life before the illness
Claire's account

Before having encephalitis in 2004, I'd had a happy, secure childhood; part of a large, loving family and many special friends. I was a brownie, guide and ranger guide and enjoyed outside activities very much. We went on great walks with our dogs in the peak district and I met and played with my friends in the local park and woodland. Shopping for me in those days was the excitement of having my two pence pocket money each Saturday morning and rushing down to "Katie's Kabin" for some sweeties (usually a Bassets liquorice stick or some aniseed balls). I now have a lovely visual memory of my dad having four two-pence coins ready for myself and my three sisters each week, and can see myself rushing down the steep hill and the pleasure of being in the old-fashioned sweetie shop where everything was in boxes and jars and the lady weighed what you wanted and gave it to you in a little paper bag.

As a teenager I happily did lots of babysitting and rose to the responsibility of being "their other mum" very well. I felt useful and special and that was very nice. I also had a job for a few hours a week washing up in the local nursing home, which I found very enjoyable and it was a positive feeling of being worthwhile. The cook usually saved me something lovely to eat after I had finished! I stopped and chatted with the residents sometimes, which was nice too. My school days were happy, with lots of friends travelling to and fro on the bus everyday—and I'm seeing it now! It cost two pence each way and I remember dad giving us each our individual piles of two-pence pieces which he had stacked up ready for all four of us on his bureau.

My parents are a nurse and doctor who met during their training at Guy's Hospital in London. My father's parents had trained there too, and I have always said that I was born a nurse and remember strongly that I was self-driven to follow in my parents' footsteps to go to Guy's myself. I was lucky to be able to go to a good school, with very motivated

teachers and they enabled this to happen for me. There was never anything else that was going to happen for me in my working life and it
meant very much to me. My memory of childhood is very patchy, but I
do still have some understanding and emotional ties to my life then, and
I was lucky to be able to go off to London at the age of 18 years to do
my General Nurse training at Guy's Hospital. I lived in the nurses' home
with the other students and quickly made friends, and enjoyed wearing
my uniform with white starched linen apron and nurse's cap, a buckled
belt and badges (Figure 5.1).

Here my memory fails me big time; I have almost none of my time
there left to remember. I have some much-practised tales about events
in that time. I can recall the words as I have told so many people the
same story over the years, but the feeling of actually being there has
completely gone. I know I made good friends with fellow student nurses
and that I had only been away from home for six weeks when my new
friend Pat and I decided to go to the fresher's ball which was happening

Figure 5.1 Claire in her nursing uniform.

for the new intake of medical students. We both happily met our lifetime partners at that event. I have said many times that I danced on Ed's feet, not that I have any memory of this actually happening but it has been a much-practised tale that I believe happened, although Ed says he can't remember! We made a very happy friendship and partnership together and had some great times at Guy's together. I know I was very happy and pleased to be training at Guy's; I loved the job, all my friends, and my wonderful partner Ed. We both qualified and chose to follow our own paths of further qualification in the areas we chose to work. Although we both lived and worked separately we did keep in very close contact together. I did further training in caring for sick children and then chose to specialise in neonatal intensive care, which I worked in for most of my 25 working years. I have now no memories of these times; I don't know where I lived and worked or who I lived with in different places, or anything about my friends at the time, but I know that I had a very happy social and working life and that Ed and I continued our wonderful partnership together (Figure 5.2). During those times I kept in regular contact with friends and family and felt happy and secure with all aspects of my life. Ed continued to move around and complete the further medical specialism he chose and we kept in very close contact.

Figure 5.2 Claire with her husband, Ed.

Which brings me to the next story! We'd been together for nine years when number one child came along rather unexpectedly. We bought a home together and settled down into a busy working family life. It got busier with children two, three and four arriving and us needing a bigger house, a people carrier and an au pair to allow me to continue working and to enjoy all the fun of my family life. Somewhere in the middle of it all, we got married!

I can barely remember anything about our wedding but have been recently reminded that our eldest son was our best man at nearly two years old and that he dug around in the plants inside the registry office and made a big mess! I am hoping to find some photos of him doing that one day.

I continued a very happy home and working life, joining in with many extra activities such as cubs and brownies, parent–teacher association, school events, and I was a very happy lady with many friends. We had very good times with our children growing up and I feel many people knew us as an active happy family.

Without ever realising just how important this was going to be to me, I happily took many photographs of these times (Figure 5.3). I have made many albums, but most of my photographs I just didn't have time to sort, and my memories are now stored in a rather chaotic fashion. I am yet to properly sort through these photos and make more meaningful

Figure 5.3 Claire, as caring as ever.

memories from them with help from my family and friends. I wish now that I had made notes when I took them, as well as notes of events that mums are meant to remember, like when their baby's first tooth fell out, when their children first spoke, what their first word was, etc. I've even got somebody's first haircut but no label to say whose it was.

My working life was very meaningful to me, I continued nursing and tried my best to give my utmost effort to every part of it and that gave my life real strength and meaning as well. Memory regarding the patients I cared for was vital to engaging effectively and safely with them. I was a very happy wife, nurse, mother, daughter, sister, auntie, cousin, work colleague, friend, etc.

Barbara has asked me to answer her pertinent question: "What kind of person was I before the illness?" Well, "Hello!" Big smile, confident body language and facial expressions, because I was always happy to greet people and be with people, to be happy together and to share our lives in appropriate and friendly, caring ways. I recognised people, knew about who they were, how we knew each other, and what parts of our lives we shared. I could happily ask to share the next instalment with them, already knowing information about them that enabled me to be caring and understanding about any difficulties they may have in their lives, and ask the right questions, sharing friendship in the most meaningful way. It is socially very important to greet people as they expect you to and I had access to lots of information regarding peoples' identity, which enabled me to know them and care about them meaningfully. When Mrs Smith said "Hello" to me in the post office I was able to remember who she was, how I knew her, some details about her life which allowed me to ask the right questions and to say the right things to her; to have the right body language and facial expressions too. I was able to live my life starting social connections with a relaxed happy smile, which I so much long for now. I knew when I went up to the school gates to collect my children, which ones they were, and I knew who many of the others belonged to, and which of the other mums to stand with or hug and which to keep clear of!

I was a happy person who knew how my Mum liked her tea, I knew how to time the eggs when my children wanted dippy eggs, I knew the lady who worked in the village shop and which of her children played with mine—and who was the best at football. I remembered when I'd arranged to help somebody else, what for and why, and the myriad of complications to be avoided to make the best job of doing it for them. I understood their behaviour and their expectations of me. There is a shared understanding that knowledge imparts, which allows us to face and manage each situation that comes along in a way appropriate for all parties involved, and I think I was well able to do this. I know that I valued memories I had made and used them in all social situations connecting with other people, but like all of us I am sure, I took them for granted without any real concept of just how vital and fundamental to engaging appropriately with others that they really are.

Before the illness, if I saw another person or heard their voice, I was able to make many decisions very quickly and succinctly about the best way to greet them, with appropriate social behaviour depending on various factors: the time of day and the place, who else was there, what time I could spare, and I knew whether I actually wanted to meet them, greet them, speak to them or otherwise. It was a myriad of important decisions involving many memories both past and present of that actual individual person. I was able to respect their needs and feelings regarding our meeting and then to behave in an appropriate way, best for both of us. I knew if I recognised them or not, knew who they were if I did, and these decisions were made very quickly almost without even realising I was doing it. It was just like that! Easy!

An ability I barely recognised has gone, and it affects my confidence and feelings of security at every single social encounter I make, in all avenues of my changed life. It's at home, at our front door, back door, in town, at the hospital, school gates, swimming pool, in the woods, car park, our own kitchen, bathroom, landing. Everywhere! I have a series of questions that I need answers to very quickly in an attempt to socialise correctly with the person in front of me. I am trying to read their mind, with mine, which isn't the easiest combination.

Are they actually looking at me? Are they just nice people being friendly? One of us sees and/or hears the other, then we make eye contact. I try to read the signs from their words, body language, facial expressions and general demeanour to try to understand something about this person, which may trigger some memory of how our lives have been shared, if at all.

I need to make many decisions from people's behaviour and I choose my most sociable attempt at reacting towards them. Somebody's near me! Are they actually looking at me or just glancing in passing? Are they moving further towards my personal space in any meaningful way? Are they widening their eyes and smiling? Or are they smiling at somebody behind me? Do they appear to wish to speak to me? Do they begin? I need to read very quickly all the inferences in both their words and body movements to ascertain their thoughts and feelings about us meeting. Somebody well known to me would usually have bright eyes, make quick eye contact, have a big smile, maybe open arms and more often than not, greet me happily by name, "Hello Claire!". People who do not wish to meet up with me would be slower with eye contact, if at all. They are unlikely to smile at me and may move their head aside to view elsewhere. They are likely to keep their arms busy with whatever they are doing and have no words towards me. Those encounters are much easier to deal with. More often than not, at my moment of uncertainty, their eye contact is brief, and passing me, they may turn away deliberately, sometimes with a half smile to themselves while they decide if they could or should be talking to me. Their arm movements may become more awkward, they may stop what they were previously doing, whilst they think. There can be muttering under their breath while they decide how best to approach me. They may begin smiling gently and say "Hello" but not greet me by name. I begin biting my tongue, hoping they are one of the few who do know me and that I'll need reminding who they are. I need to read every aspect of their behaviour towards me to try and comprehend whether they have any past or present knowledge about me.

I try to appear happy to see them, and friendly in a rather untrue way. All I really want to say is, "Who are you? How do I know you? What do you know about me? (And when are you going to get your bloody moustache out of my ear!)" I'm biting my tongue and hoping they are one of those individuals who know that I'll need reminding who they are. I carry on speaking with them and listening, all the time hoping that a moment may come when I may be able to jog them into realising that I don't know who they are without actually asking. But just the act of smiling back, greeting and then meaningless chatting, having accepted their social advance, tends to infer to them that I do know them. They may see me as the same Claire as before the illness. Nothing physical gives me away except my hunched shoulders and ribbed forehead, and I'm still able to widen my eyes and pretend to smile such that I appear to be friendly towards them.

The thoughtfulness and caring which keeps friendships alive relies deeply on understanding. The words of my Nana come to mind: ". . . the best way to have friends is to be one". I realise now just how very valuable the evocation of memories is in all manner of social connections with everyone around us. True friendship involves being one and being one is something I managed without having to worry too much about what memories I needed to find to care meaningfully about others. It just happened.

I remembered important details of each of my children's worlds and what made them the characters they were then. I understood how they *chose to live their lives, who they chose to share it with and in what ways. My understanding enabled me to care for them and to show my love for them in a meaningful way. It helped me to live happily with them, to congratulate them for "raising to pointe" in the ballet show or winning the sack race at sports day, and it allowed me to share those memories happily with them and with Ed and our friends.*

Barbara's comments: We can see from this account that Claire had a busy, fulfilling life. She enjoyed her work, her family and her friends. There is obviously no sign of any physical or mental health problems. This was all to change when the Herpes simplex virus attacked Claire, causing her to have HSVE, which led to parts of her brain being destroyed and leaving her with numerous cognitive problems including prosopagnosia. She also has a fairly severe and lengthy loss of memory for the years before her encephalitis. This is known as retrograde amnesia (RA) and can vary from a few minutes, seen in some survivors of traumatic brain injury, to decades in others, such as those with Korsakoff's syndrome (Wilson, 2009). Ribot's law (1881) states that recent memories are lost first with oldest memories being most resistant to disruption. This is not always true, however, especially for those with encephalitis (Kopelman, Stanhope, & Kingsley, 1999). Claire seems to have an incomplete RA gap of many years although she retains some islands of memory during those years. Her major problem though is her loss of knowledge about people. She has forgotten their essential characteristics, their identity and this is what is so heartbreaking for her.

Chapter 6

Calling my husband Stephanie

In April 2004 I was a busy working mum aged 43, happily married, and we had four healthy, happy children, then aged eight, ten, thirteen and fifteen, two boys and two girls, not forgetting the rabbit, the snakes and the cats! I have no memory of this happening, but I am told I'd had a couple of days being unwell with a temperature, cold and flu-like symptoms, a headache and unusual dreams for a few days. Also, I'd had some days off work, which I'm still surprised that I can't remember, as it was so rare for me to have to do this. I'm told that I became gradually worse over these few days, and became increasingly confused. Apparently, I was behaving quite oddly and my family were becoming quite worried about me. Our daughter told me afterwards that I'd called my husband "Stephanie", which helped clinch the decision to get me some help. I was taken to our local hospital and quickly treated with medication, and then I was transferred to Intensive Care at a larger hospital some way away. I had slipped into a coma by this time. I was diagnosed with Herpes simplex viral encephalitis and treated with IV acyclovir. An MRI scan was carried out at that time.

The virus had somehow managed to cross the barrier from blood to brain and caused severe inflammation of the brain tissue. I am told I had seizures at this time. Not being able to remember has its uses sometimes!

So there I was—miles away from home, in a coma, in hospital, with no real reassurance for my family that I would survive. Whatever must it have been like for them? Our youngest daughter was only eight years old! Our eldest son was just about to sit his GCSE exams (General Certificate of Secondary Education exams, which are public examinations taken by British school children) and all of them needed a great deal of help to support them through this difficult time. I am told I was in a deep coma for four weeks and then in and out for another three. I am told that many kind people visited me during this time. Thankfully, somebody made me a visitor's book, and kept all my get well soon cards, all of which are very precious to me now. I wasn't able to thank them, or know they had been to visit me. This has been very upsetting. Ed brought our children to visit me regularly and I have lovely notes kept from them. It was at one of those visits that I'm told I made my first meaningful word after all that time being unable to respond. I had been in hospital for about seven weeks and one of our sons spoke to me from a place where I couldn't see him and I said his name. They must all have been so delighted and relieved, just to know that "I" was still there—wife, mum, Claire.

My family and friends were very upset when I did come round but was unable to recognise or understand who anybody was. I know I was very confused during those times and realise now that my visitors understood the explanations given to them to some extent but that it was a long time before I had any concept of them myself. My earliest memories are of having frightening dreams, mostly involving my husband, Ed, who seemed a completely strange person I was very scared of. He wasn't nasty to me in any way in the dreams, but I was very distressed having no understanding of who he was any more. Even worse, though, was waking up and finding it real. I am relieved now to think that at least he was able to understand my confusion and to allow for it. I remember my feelings of fear and emptiness but no details of how we responded to each other at that time. Thankfully, I have his lovely messages in my visitor's book and I do know my fear was forgiven. One message said "Hello, Claire—today you have been very talkative, which is great. The best moment was when you told me and two of your friends that you wanted to know 'where all the interesting people had gone?' I love you to bits, Edxxx."

Although I didn't have any idea that we had four children, and didn't recognise any of them, I think my strong maternal instinct was able to help me to try and believe who I was being told they were. They all visited me regularly and I have great warmth reading their messages too. Memories! Their value is a secure and unbelievable reassurance for me now. "Hello, Mummy! We all came and visited you today and you smiled at me when I said I loved you!" "This time you are extremely better and I am extremely happy." "I'm waiting for the coming home day. Miss you loads." "I imagine it won't be long before you come home and we can all have lunch together. Love you lots xxx."

I know that my main feelings were distress and confusion and that it was a long time before I had any concept of prosopagnosia myself, or how it was affecting my thinking. I could see faces. I knew they were faces but they were all strangers to me. I have lost a huge bank of factual *and emotional information about my own life and I have almost noth-ing of anyone else's either. I was surrounded by a sea of unknown faces which had no meaning to me.*

People just smiling and waving at me are really complicated. It is not much fun having an unknown lady smiling at you but it helps when she says "Hi, Claire, I'm your mum." However, she could have been one of the hospital staff coming to ask me something or Sally, who I used to work with, coming to visit me. I try not to make immediate eye contact with people until I am sure that they are trying to make eye contact with me. This has mainly prevented me from happily greeting someone else's visitors with "Hello, Dad" or from people thinking I am being nosey because I am looking at them. But not making immediate eye contact with those who expect me to can make me seem uncaring, aloof or just unfriendly.

Barbara's comments: We know that Claire was admitted to hospital in May 2004. While there, she had an MRI scan, which showed damage in the right temporal lobe, extending into the adjacent basal ganglia, insula and inferior frontal lobe. Limited high signal change was also evident in the left temporal lobe (see Figure 2.1).

The virus had caused damage to several parts of the brain, particularly in the right temporal lobe, an area crucially involved in face processing. Claire was treated with aciclovir, one of the most commonly used anti-viral drugs. Granerod and Crowcroft (2007) suggest that, if given early enough, aciclovir dramatically reduces the mortality and the morbidity of the disease. The drug may save lives and reduce the extent of the ensuing problems but does not stop all damage to the brain. Along with some 25% of survivors of encephalitis, Claire also suffered from seizures although the frequency of these has now reduced considerably.

In an interview with Ed, in January 2014, he explained what had happened: "She had a quite nasty gastro-intestinal upset and that's all it seemed to be. She had a fever at one point, the GI upset for a couple of days which didn't seem to recover. And then after a couple of days she went to the GPs surgery just like you would normally, although we usually try to avoid going to the surgery when we've got something like that. And they didn't think there was anything else wrong either. Then, perhaps, a day after that, she told me that she was having very peculiar dreams—but again, she'd been pyrexial (high temperature) so it wasn't anything especially out of the ordinary. She didn't really elaborate on that which is a pity as it sounds like they probably were quite weird and she can't remember now. Then there was the Stephanie incident and we thought that's really strange and . . . then we took her in." She went quite quickly downhill. So between getting into hospital and becoming unconscious was just a few hours.

She was in ITU (intensive treatment unit) for seven days of which about three of those she didn't recover consciousness at all . . . and then, for the last three or four, she did occasionally wake up and was able to take herself to the loo but she wouldn't have been in the least bit aware of what was going on and she scribbled a couple of random things on her chart. So she wasn't in a coma at that point but completely unaware and in a deep sleep. She woke for a few minutes. And then she left neuro ITU and was on the ward. She wasn't any way in a coma but she was unaware of what was happening. When she said her son's name, it would have been one of the first times the children went to see her and she was awake and conversing so it would have been after a few weeks, I couldn't tell you exactly but I would think two to three weeks when that happened.

At that point, of course, we didn't know how deep her prosopagnosia was although we knew she wasn't recognising people. There was one point where there was a ward round so there were a number of people standing around the bed and I was one of them and the consultant asked her to point me out—which she did but then almost immediately couldn't, so she said who I was but then 30 seconds later she'd lost me even though I hadn't moved. That would have been around the same time.

Barbara asked Ed if he thought then that Claire was going to be OK. He said, "Not necessarily. It seemed as if it was possible she was going to get OK again but I hadn't really seen—or I didn't have a good appreciation of what the scans showed, so I didn't know. I had a broad idea of what the possibilities were. But I'm sure everyone says this—you get caught up in the practicalities. So—well, certainly I do in situations like that. I didn't think whether it was awful for me or not. You have to go to work, you have to sort the children out, you have to bring the children here every weekend so your life changes but I think you just get so deeply into dealing with the situation. I did make a decision quite early to concentrate on making sure the children were OK even if it meant saying, 'well today I can't do anything for Claire', or worrying about her well being first, because I thought that is what she would want me to do. So I sort of concentrated on the children's well being, their emotional and coping mechanisms, more than worrying about her."

Chapter 7

Kissing a cauliflower

Ed has told me that one day, while I was in hospital, he was feeding me, and offered me a piece of cauliflower (which I love) on a fork. I leant forward and kissed it! I was awake in hospital feeling very lost, confused, and disorientated in my surroundings. I had awoken into a world I knew nothing about. The first I knew about anything was being told I'd had a virus seven weeks ago. I know that it was some time before I had any concept of the consequences of the illness myself. I didn't initially realise that I was unable to recognise or remember anybody's identity. I had bad dreams regarding people's identity during that time. A neuropsychological assessment identified that I had problems with memory, both long term and short term, lack of facial recognition, prosopagnosia, problems with word recognition and retrieval, verbal abstraction, speed of cognition, and visuo-spatial skills. The results also showed that I was severely anxious.

So what did that mean to me? Here I was, being told that I was somebody who I knew nothing about; that this man "Ed" was my husband, and that these four children were ours. I knew nothing about any of them and couldn't recognise anybody. I had no understanding of my life, where I lived, worked, or who I shared it with. Words can't describe just how lost and confused I felt. My family were strangers to me. Whatever it must have been like for them I can't imagine. It was very hard for me to accept that these strangers were my family. I think I was able to believe that the children were mine, from a strong maternal instinct, but it was very difficult to feel the same confidence to re-bond with Ed. I told myself to believe that as I had married him, this man must be the right man for me, even if I didn't know anything about either of us anymore.

I was told that one of the strangers was my husband, others were my own children, friends and wider family. They all came to visit me, to love and support me, the me I used to be, but how could I pretend to be the me they had come to see? I was alive in a life I knew nothing about, getting big smiles, presents and hugs from people I knew even less about, with no real sense of belonging. I have no idea who visited me, even if I were told at the time it meant nothing to me. Identity is not just a name, it involves a whole wealth of circumstances around a person and appreciation of how their lives have been shared with mine. "Hello, Claire, I'm Sally!" means nothing to me.

I have lovely meaningful words written by friends and family about their experiences of those times and they do really make me feel part of it. My dad says: "My most lasting memory is of the first day that we came to see you in hospital—you must have been a patient for several days. You were in the High Dependency unit and were, to all intents and purposes, unconscious but you would show several moments of responding to what we said to you." Mum has also written about this visit: "You were very sleepy and we would say, 'Claire, Claire, can you hear me? It's your Mum and Dad.' You opened your eyes and they looked strikingly blue but you were so sleepy and uncomprehending. On another visit you are in a ward, more awake and talking to us, your Mum and Dad. You are learning your way around the ward. You have to cross a corridor to the toilets and, at first, you need someone with you. Tiny steps each day over many weeks. On another visit I come with Anne-Marie, we say who we are and gently try to jog your memory. Not too much, though, as it distresses you. We give you a warm blue cardigan, you like it even if you forget where it comes from. You are pleased it comes from your Mum and Dad (and you still wear it). You tell us you are going to Occupational Therapy. They take you to a kitchen in the hospital and you have to show you can find your way around a kitchen, understand recipes and be able to cook safely. You know you can't go home until the doctors are satisfied that you can manage on your own. You still can't remember faces. One day we are sitting in the hospital garden and along the path comes Ed. You don't know him. 'Is that Ed? They tell me he's my husband.' You tell us the children visit you and you are trying to remember them. Eventually, you seem to accept that Ed is your husband and you have children and a home. You try going home for a weekend at first. We talk to you on the phone. I can't remember when you first remembered my voice but you certainly do now."

It is lovely to have these letters and to be able to re-read their memories of a time completely unknown to me. And I have lots of my own scribbled words on pieces of paper and notebooks which are helpful too. One describes my sister and mother-in-law having a laugh together when my sister was washing my hair and tidying me up one day, saying "I'm the oldest, do as I say." She explained that it was something we used to say when we were children. Number one, number two! We all had a laugh together.

I can't tell you how special it feels just being able to visualise these moments. Although I can't visualise the actual place or any of the people involved, I do have a very real sense of belonging to these written events which feels very good. It makes me realise and feel like I've come a very long way since then.

I have a few very patchy memories of my childhood, up to the age of 18, and struggle with the next 25 years of my life with almost complete amnesia. I have lost a bank of factual information, semantic memory, and consequently a lot of confidence. I don't understand humour and sarcasm anymore, and have verbal communication misunderstanding, which gives me emotional anxiety. I am generally anxious about not understanding my past, not appreciating the present, and confusion about the future. This leads to difficulty sleeping and worrisome dreams. I get very over tired which makes me less able to find confidence to manage the situations I find myself in. I have extreme noise sensitivity and struggle to manage loud or sudden noises, and particular pitches. I have difficulty tolerating bright lights and any changes with lights going on and off is very disturbing. I have occasionally had seizures since my discharge from hospital especially if faced with flashing lights and particular sounds. A seizure almost occurred when I heard African drumming at a music concert. Fortunately, I was able to leave the concert in time to prevent it happening but another survivor of encephalitis who was with me at the time and in a wheelchair did not manage to escape in time and did have a seizure. For me, if I hear high pitches and a fast beat, I can still feel the beginnings of seizure feelings so I remove myself.

During my time in hospital I was given very helpful knowledge of my difficulties and much support to help me to understand them and work towards ways to help myself manage them. I had a lot of help from various different people with specialist support for each separate type of difficulty. The neuropsychologist, Bonnie-Kate, helped me particularly with the prosopagnosia and much of my emotional difficulties. I will say more about her in the next chapter. The occupational therapist helped me with attention problems and executive functioning and the speech and language therapist with misunderstandings of words and their meanings.

My journey through rehabilitation had begun! Staff knew about my difficulties coping with the changes in my life and were very kind, caring and supportive at all times. And so were all my family, very much. Whatever must it have been like for them to have all the happiness and relief of "me" back, but at the same time I was not at all the same "me" anymore? I didn't know anything about them, and I had forgotten about some basic living skills—how to eat, how to find my way to the bathroom, where anything I needed was kept. I am very grateful to the person who provided me a visitor's book and I have many lovely messages from my family and friends, right from day one. Just reading their words about what happened and how I was managing has helped me have a real understanding of just how frightening it must have been for all of them.

I have very happy and positive messages from my husband and children, my wider family and many lovely friends and ex-workmates. Just reading through these words gives me a real sense of belonging to a time I otherwise know nothing about, and it has really helped me. I find the written word gives me a great sense of security.

I did a lot of writing with the various therapists who looked after me and was encouraged to use strategies to help me to manage. It felt very embarrassing and frustrating to re-learn skills but writing things down myself really helped. I felt then, and still do now that written instructions, plans, etc. have safety, and provide memories for me which I can access easily. This is very reassuring.

The staff taught me how to use planned routines to enable me to complete tasks, to organize my actions carefully and in an appropriate order. I was encouraged to take time and think carefully through what I was doing, how and why. I have kept many notebooks in which I have written at length. I was taught how to take ten deep breaths, to take my time and avoid rushing things which made me over tired. I used lists to help myself plan my actions, to remember things to do, and what order to do them in. I had written directions to help me get to places I needed to be. The occupational therapists helped me hugely to regain confidence and some feelings of positive self-worth again as I became more able to manage as time went on.

The speech and language therapists helped me with word-finding techniques as I was struggling to remember the names of objects and how to continue a conversation meaningfully even if I am unable to use the exact word. They, too, gave me confidence to manage each day in a more positive way. They supported me in describing a word, often being enough for the listener to guess the target word themselves. They reassured me that I do not need to provide every word for a conversation to continue. I also needed reminding about turn taking.

I have bad difficulties understanding humour and sarcasm and tend to take things too literally very often without realizing that somebody is *joking. This has also been very difficult for me, as I already have low self-confidence, so I think that many people may be saying bad things around me. I was encouraged to look out for body language, facial expression, tone and intonation of the person's speech and their general body positioning to help assess what they are actually meaning. This was difficult for me at the beginning, but it became even more difficult over the years, as all four of our children have travelled through teenage years together and continue to have lots of fun with language as all healthy people learn to do in happy social connections. I'm just not learning quite so quickly.*

Barbara's comment: Ed talked about Claire's loss of sarcasm and humour too. He said "She completely lost her ability to understand sarcasm and humour. This was a major problem and still is a little bit. So every single word she hears, she hears the literal meaning. Not so much anymore. Even if she doesn't understand the sarcasm any more, or the humour in it, she does understand that such a thing exists and people might be using it. For a house full of four teenagers who were routinely used to using it a lot, it's not easy. Mostly it was negative statements between siblings. They'd be saying something rude about each other but with smiles on their faces, and so we would all know it was teasing or gentle—it would be anything, anything like that and you don't realise how much, I certainly didn't realise how much, we operate using those very subtle linguistic clues and there's so much she didn't understand. This is all mixed in with the identity thing and the prosopagnosia. We've said to her, you know you can tell in someone's eyes whether they are being serious or not serious and you can tell, you can know, from the context. We know that we are not being horrible to each other because we know that we are not 'horrible to each other' people and so, you take it for granted, if someone says something horrible, if it's someone you're secure with. If they say something horrible then it's probably sarcastic. That's all gone for her because she doesn't have that identity of the person, including us, so she spent a long time thinking we were being terrible to each other and we didn't really realise for a while how significant that was. But on another level, when you sit down and say 'Do you really believe we were being that horrible to each other because you know we're not nasty people?' she says, 'No, I know. I know you're not horrible people.' That was a massive difficulty".

During life we become semi-prepared for awful health problems by either hearing about them or visualizing people suffering from them. No healthy person really knows what it must be like to be blind, have cancer or be unable to walk but we do have some concept of these difficulties—and at least we have heard of them and may have had the experience of knowing someone with this problem, so have knowledge of their journey through it.

I woke up in hospital, being told I had been there for seven weeks. I didn't know anything about myself or any of my family and didn't recognize any of them. Think of a person known to you—all manner of oddments of information will come to mind to acknowledge that person's identity. You know all kinds of important and trivial things about that person's character and lifestyle.

I had completed 25 years of nursing, caring for all kinds of patients with many difficulties, but I had absolutely no concept of what it might be like to wake up one day and not even know yourself as an individual, let alone anyone else around you, even your parents, husband, children. I was totally unprepared to have no understanding of my life. The idea that I had crash-landed into somebody else's life gave me some vague way of thinking about how it felt.

Home! That is where I have come to, to my own family and my own life and, although I am still unable to recognise faces or understand anything regarding their identity, I'd been very well supported by the therapists in hospital who had taught me very useful strategies to use to help myself manage these worries, and many others.

My body has survived but my brain does not know me anymore. I appear normal to others and my kind family and friends wish to judge me as normal. It was very hard for them to realise and understand just how much my feelings of normality have been broken. There was a life which once was mine and now, over time, I need to learn all about it again. Many aspects of ourselves form our own identity—our parents, our childhood, our wider family, friends, school life and going out into the big wide world and what happens then. We take on responsibilities and have hopes and personal direction for our lives. We find partners, have a family, enjoy different activities, music, food and all have our own likes and dislikes which form our character, make us ourselves. We have knowledge of a world we live in and share with others, we have knowledge and belief in our past lives and have aspirations for our future. I am expected to know just who I am, how I exist, how I live, but nobody gave me the plan. The whole time when I was awake in hospital was very confusing and upsetting but I was aware that although I was not understanding anything, people were trying to be kind to me. I felt that they were giving their support to me and caring about my troubles. All the staff and the various therapists did their work calmly and made me *feel secure and understood which helped hugely. They taught me about cauliflowers too!*

But I have survived! I have not died although the person lost is me. Encephalitis has taken away my own identity and that of everyone else around me. Worse than that, everyone around me had their own expectations of the "me" I was meant to be. They knew themselves, each other, the me I was supposed to be—the me they thought of as me. They all knew about what was happening around us and gave kind explanations to me and lots of reassurance which meant nothing to me. It was very frightening for me just not knowing who I needed to pretend to be.

In the postcode lottery of life I was in the right place at exactly the right time to have received the best possible care available—the exceptional vision and support given by the expert team at the hospital and for the best Neuro Rehab I hit the jackpot—Barbara Wilson! She and her expert team have enabled me to survive mentally as best I possibly could have, and my being is still continuing to become clearer each day thanks to all of them. Barbara gave me Bonnie-Kate Dewar who gave me so much understanding over a long period of time and then I was able to have six months neuro-rehabilitation at the Oliver Zangwill Centre. I can't even begin to tell you how much it has helped me to know, feel like and be me. But here I go!

Barbara's comments: While in hospital, Claire was in touch with Bonnie-Kate Dewar, a neuropsychologist working with me in Cambridge. The initial assessment was carried out in June 2004 when it was found that Claire had problems with memory, facial recognition, word recognition and retrieval, verbal abstraction, speed of cognition and visuo-spatial skills.

Bonnie-Kate and Claire established a good rapport; they continued to see each other when Claire was discharged. Ed brought Claire in regularly for outpatient appointments. One of the things Claire remembers clearly from her neuropsychological appointments was Bonnie-Kate saying "Together we can."

It was Bonnie-Kate who discussed with me whether to make the referral to the Oliver Zangwill Centre (OZC). We decided this would be beneficial to Claire; the referral was made in September 2004 and the initial one day assessment to see if the OZC programme would be appropriate for Claire, and that Claire would be willing to attend the centre, took place in December 2004. This assessment is described in Appendix 1.

Chapter 8

Together we can

Neuropsychologist Bonnie-Kate Dewar spent many valuable times with me explaining how and why my autobiographical memory was so severely impaired, why I had such profound amnesia about my life and why I was struggling so hugely to encode new memories of what was happening then. She gave me great help to understand the consequences of my illness and made me feel that it was normal, accepted, expected and alright for me to feel so awful. She helped me to accept my changed circumstances to some extent and together we worked through valuable ways for me to adjust to the changes. One of the problems noticed when I had the neuropsychological assessment was prosopagnosia.

Prosopagnosia tends to be initially described to people as "having no facial recognition". Sadly, it's much deeper than that; not only do I not recognize somebody's face but I struggle to have any memory of their identity. I don't know anything about them, anything about their lives, how we know each other, or what parts of our lives we have shared. They're a stranger to me. When they happily tell me their name—"I'm Sally!", "I'm Linda!", "I'm Christopher!"—they think that's enough for me and they feel happy that I'm reminded who they are. But a name isn't everything. How many Linda's do I know? Have I worked with a Sally? Is Christopher my son? A name does not give identity and not having the helpful prompt of recognizing someone's face leaves me panicking about who this person is, and how to react to them appropriately.

The explanation "face-blindness" tends to give the idea that once I have been given a person's name that will be all that I need. Sadly, the difficulties only start there, as I have a whole loss of understanding about their identity and a name doesn't mean everything. They are strangers. Whether I was told their name two minutes ago, this morning, yesterday or last week, they remain a stranger to me regardless of how well we once knew each other. Their features don't tell me anything about their identity. I am unable to see a person behind the curtain of features, which I know I can see, but they mean nothing to me. We have all got two eyes, a nose, a mouth, hair, neck, ears and so on but to me there is no story attached to the combination that is apparent to me. To "me"? Bonnie-Kate gave me huge understanding and support to manage my difficulties and consequent feelings of much confusion and unhappiness. She made me feel safe that my reactions to what was happening were normal, and her great words, which gave me much strength, were "together we can . . ." Having somebody understand how it felt, supported me and would help me to find ways to manage things was so reassuring. I've never been a person to share my innermost feelings with others, but she was there with me and it did feel like we were together, which was really great at a time I felt so alone and detached from a world I'd lost all sense of belonging in.

Bonnie-Kate helped me to feel better, and more in control of my feelings using goal management training to manage my anxiety and improve my own sense of managing life. I needed to re-learn simple ways of doing things and use strategies to remember them. She helped me to think straight (I think the proper word for this is "cognition" and I was understanding that I had misunderstandings of this). She looked at ways to help challenge my thinking to increase my coping skills and reduce my anxiety. I had many strict rules with myself, ingrained into my behaviour, and I needed support to think through my thoughts and actions in order to make sure that I was making the right choices of how to manage different aspects of my life, what still worked, and what needed altering now that my coping skills were changed. She helped me to identify my assumptions and enabled me to alter some of my own strict rules. I was encouraged to use written notes and lists to help me to remember different plans and series of actions. She asked me to consider different ways of managing difficulties, thinking through the differing outcomes and then do some positive planning myself. I very quickly began to RELY completely on written notes, which gave me a huge sense of security about life, and a great increase in my own confidence to manage better.

Bonnie-Kate worked with me with faces of photographs of people who I used to know and recognize, some famous faces, and some who I never have known. These were difficult and I struggled to feel any real improvement with these and mainly used another item on the photo to try and remember which one was which, rather than who was who. We worked through various different ways of seeing if my prosopagnosia may have improved. I was given a number of faces to see and then to say who I thought they might be. I wasn't able to recognise the faces but I did learn how to cheat and to recognise the photos!

Barbara's comment: Oh Claire, that was clever of you and you fooled us, we thought you were learning to recognise some of the faces . . . Researchers beware!

I was learning a huge amount at that time and becoming very aware that I needed other aspects of vision to rely upon to try and identify somebody rather than their facial features. Bonnie-Kate understood the extent of my difficulties and tried various methods to help me, but the main thing which helped me hugely was her understanding, her kindness and her endless compassion.

We worked on mnemonics to help me to connect with someone's identity from their visual appearance and I found these very useful strategies to help jog a memory, as this helped me to retrieve information about a person. Here is an example of one of them, which I still use now, ten years later. I have a lovely friend who I don't recognize anytime, anywhere, but I know that she has long curly blonde hair, and also that she lives in a lane called "Golden Drop". I connect her long blonde curls with Golden Drop and when I meet her in the village I have a good hope of seeing curls and they trigger the mnemonic of "Golden Drop", which enables me to appreciate her identity more quickly. I know somebody else as "Pat the egg man" and visualizing his home and him carrying some eggs enables me to remember his identity too. The mnemonics worked well for a few individuals I knew very well, but it was not possible to cover enough individuals who I was in regular contact with throughout my time in hospital and after discharge. My husband, Ed, wears a shark's tooth necklace, which enables me to know who he is and feel secure just around the house or anywhere else in life.

I was lucky to be looked after by many staff and have many visitors. I have several gifts which were given and a box of cards which I still haven't yet ventured to open, knowing it will be very emotional reading, kind and loving messages from unknown people. The one thing I treasured at that time, and still do, is a poem written for me by my friend's mum and I do remember that it really felt as though I had an identity of my own in the middle of everything happening: "Hello Claire, my name is Jeanne, we are all very keen, to help you through your present plight, we all love you Claire with all our might." The poem was a real starting point for me to understand that something had happened to me, and her words of love and warmth towards me made me appreciate my confusion regarding my own identity, let alone anyone else's. That was a real start!

I was a real person and I began to imagine a few details about who I was—and to learn some details too. Well everyone else seemed to know! My family and friends happily shared memories of a life with "me" in it, which I had lost. I had felt so strangely separated from "myself" but everyone else seems to have their concepts and memories of "me" and they happily reminded me.

Somebody kindly started a visitor's book and I have many lovely messages from people and their encouragement as to how to manage my feelings better. My husband and children have written beautiful messages in it. I suddenly remembered that I have already told you about it! That shows you how special it is. "Claire, honeybunch, this is just to remind you that everybody is writing you messages in this book when they come to visit you. We all hope that this will help you remember things. At the moment remembering things is difficult for you."

Over the last few weeks in hospital the letters all said how I was improving and I know it was from everyone's continued help and support as well as my own drive to get well again. I was allowed home for the day once or twice, and then for a weekend, which I know was a total mixture of excitement and fear. I had no sense of belonging to my family, they all knew and understood each other and they interacted together in a way I couldn't hope to keep up with. They were clearly a very happy working unit who were very confident together. They were all complete strangers to me, strangers with expectations of the "me" they hoped I'd still be. But I didn't know anything about "me" either. I was very nervy, jumped at the slightest noise and spent a large part of the time crying. It was just the same when I was finally discharged home.

I came home to a house where I could not find my way around or know where anything was kept. Apparently I threw a whole load of my clothing away not believing it was mine. I didn't recognise anybody, which added to my memory problems, yet I was wife, mum, friend and daughter. I needed to make my best efforts to try to re-fit into those roles. Inside the house, I had a great deal of support but outside was much harder. How many children rush out of the school gates to a group of happily smiling parents greeting them at the end of the day? Mine came out to a mum who had to rely on them to give me the message that they were mine—in a muddle of all the other children who also knew me and were greeting me, let alone all the other parents and friends doing the same. One of the other lads' fathers told his son that he thought I was very shy. But "shy" is something I don't think I ever was before.

I know that my family were very upset themselves to find me like this but they stuck together and supported each other as well as me. I can't *really imagine just what it must have been like for them to manage to cope with this awful situation, but they did. And I put this down to my lovely husband, as I know that right from the beginning he felt that out of the six of us, the children would be the ones to need the most emotional support to protect their feelings, and I am sure he has been right. I had to believe that they were my husband and children but they suddenly had their wife/mum not recognizing them and not knowing anything about them individually or anything about our lives together. They made notes for me, and lists and made sure they told me how to help them properly and were very kind and understanding when I needed help, or did things wrong. I found pink heart-shaped post-it notes all around the house to help me. "Bedroom", "Bathroom", "Tea bags", "I love you mummy", amongst others.*

Ed's memory of Claire going home from hospital: "She clearly didn't remember the house and it became very quickly clear that if she was to go outside the house, she'd be lost. We went immediately on a lovely holiday, everyone had a nice time. Actually, I think Claire still remembers parts of that because it was such an unusual holiday. We went to France. We stayed in a water mill, an old water mill. It was a very unusual—a very distinct thing to remember and we took lots of photos and things. That was when I started to realise the full nature of the disabilities. How can I illustrate? Again, really probably a memory thing but she always liked reading maps so when we were driving through France we gave her the map and that turned out to be a big mistake because she kept forgetting where we were going and what we were doing—that was just upsetting her so in the end we had to take the map away and give it to someone else. It was difficult—she kept saying where are we going, what road are we on?

I have always said that "I was born a nurse" and have always loved children, and I know that being a mum was, and still is, a very special part of my life. But it wasn't easy. I was in an unknown world, one where all of the parameters had changed. I was at home. I didn't know myself or anyone else. I couldn't recognize animals/birds either and even now, years later my family still remember and remind me happily that I named everything as a giraffe! I had no concept of gender initially and had to re-learn ways to appreciate this; skin colouring and nationality confused me too. I do have very muddled memories of approaching a very dark-skinned gentleman believing he was Ed and he kindly directed me to where Ed was sitting. I get startled by mirrors and don't even recognize myself in them. Going into the department stores in the city centre was, and still is, hard as I struggle to realize that the dressed-up models aren't real people, or the pixies and tigers! I jump out of my skin and feel very wary in that environment—even little hedgehog planters in the garden centre shock me.

Talking about going places reminds me to tell you that I continued to have occasional seizures after I had been discharged home, and was unable to drive for a long period of time. Not very useful for my family! Let alone not being able to cook for them, look after them and understand them; I couldn't even be "Mum's taxi" anymore. None of that helped our relationships together and these times were very problematic for all of us.

I still needed to understand all about home-life and how I fitted in. I was overwhelmed by being unfamiliar with everybody and everything I wanted to do. My family tried very hard to help me but to me it made me feel cancelled, un-needed and left out. I was told "We managed perfectly well when you were in hospital" which was meant to make me feel better but made me think I'd had no value beforehand, as well as feeling that I had even less now.

Barbara's comment: Ed mentioned there were difficulties when Claire came home. He said "Initially, our oldest daughter had to do all the cooking, lots of other preparation, school preparation. I had to take on all the things that Claire had done. Those are just practical things. When she came home there were, for quite a few years, quite a few difficulties and clashes between the children and her which were normal in a way, I suppose because our oldest daughter had done all the cooking and organising and had managed very well, actually. Then Claire came back and was unable to think of the children as anything other than being very young. So that created difficulties when our oldest daughter wanted to do something and she wasn't allowed even though she'd been doing it—simple things like using the microwave. I think our youngest would have been nine or so and she wanted to go to the cinema with her friends and Claire wasn't allowing her. Those were the kind of clashes that we had. They really related to her insecurity about everything and her anxiety about everything. For the first few years her prosopagnosia wasn't, from our point of view, ever a problem. If you asked us what was the main problem, the actual face recognition, the prosopagnosia, in its completely limited definition, was never something we really thought about. Except that we realised she wouldn't recognise anybody that came in. But for us we knew that after a while she knew who we were. She was able to, mostly, have an idea of who her kids were though she might not know which one was which. So the actual recognition thing wasn't for us such a problem as the horrendous anxiety, the crying all the time, and much more difficulty when it came to identity. So it's that which would have been so much more important, her inability to link up names of people to her past and her understanding of who they were and her history with them was a cause of great distress as I am sure she's said. She doesn't say this much anymore, but she used to say to me that she didn't feel like she was the same person. She didn't mean just memory. She meant that she had a strange disconnect between who her brain was telling her she was and who she thought she actually was—which is terribly difficult to put into words. So that's Claire's identity problem. That took up a lot of time and took us a long time to understand as well. No, that's not fair. We understood what the problem was but it took us a long time to understand how deeply affected by it she was."

I have understood something since then that may have helped me at the time, and that's that the frontal lobe of our brain doesn't mature naturally until we are 18 to 20 and it's this part of our brain which enables us to understand, appreciate other people's needs and feelings. Yet we expect teenagers to show some care in the world, but they don't have the actual ability to understand others completely. We do not expect a baby to talk, a four-year-old to pass A-levels[1], but we do expect teenagers to care rather more than we should. So there was I with a damaged frontal lobe and children piling into their teenage years. It was never going to be easy for any of us. And poor Ed, who's ended up having to be the referee, desperately trying not to take sides, supports all of us and tries to hold the whole family together.

After discharge I was lucky to be able to be return to the hospital as an outpatient and continue to see the same neuropsychologist, Bonnie-Kate Dewar, who had helped me in hospital. She understood all about my difficulties and listened and helped by teaching me good coping strategies. She helped with all my home life stresses and relationships there, and continued to work with me on my problems with prosopagnosia generally. I was encouraged to have time to rest, and to make myself stop and do it, which has never been easy for me but she did encourage me to try. She appreciated the whole feeling of my loss of self, my loss of my own identity, which used to be so shared with others and its loss now made me feel completely alone. She knew that so much of our relationships are dependent on our memories and our history with people, so she was able to give me huge understanding and support about how I felt. We discussed the difficulties and did problem solving work to help me to understand how I might be able to manage better. Every meeting was very valuable to me, and it felt very secure being in the company of somebody who really understood and cared. And she wrote and posted a letter with everything we'd covered, and our plans of action, which arrived in the post the next day! "See your social situation as something you can manage rather than something that controls and overwhelms you." It was fantastic to have it written down, and I trusted that the advice and support was safe. I could re-read it whenever I liked, and still read it sometimes now. Bonnie-Kate had written her advice, and the strategies I was to try and use, this really helped me to solve the problems and to learn how to make life easier for all of us.

Together we began my Friendship Book "to help replace my wonderful memories back to their special and rightful places". She helped me to form this notebook to store memories of my friendships in safety and where I could access them easily when I wanted to remember something, where she helped me to write and keep special information about people which re-jigged some memories and replaced the lost ones.

It was not easy being at home, and to make it worse, I was also having to cope with appointments at Occupational Health regarding my employment as a nurse and how I might manage this again. I was very anxious and became very tearful. Their team was very supportive and kind but I needed to face my difficulties regarding responsibilities for safety in my work role. I remembered and felt wholeheartedly that the safety and well being of patients in my care was vital. I realised and understood that I was no longer able to take responsibility for the best care they deserved any more. It was very upsetting for me but I was able to see just how vulnerable my patients would be. As well as not recognising them and possibly mistaking their needs, I don't think very clearly or quickly enough to have confidence to manage effectively or safely. After months of regular occupational health appointments I was put on ill-health retirement but the consultant did say kindly to me "I'm not saying that you can't do anything." However, my work-related identity was lost. I had been a nurse, SRN (State Registered Nurse), RSCN (Registered Sick Children's Nurse), ENB405 qualification (English National Board 405 refers to Special and Intensive Care of the Newborn), caring for people as best I could and hoping to make their lives better, but I'm not that Claire anymore and I had to accept it. It was around this time when I was starting to venture into the social world again, when I was introduced to somebody—"This is Claire. She was our nurse." And that said it ALL! WAS. I can't say I am a nurse anymore, and that has broken my heart. All I wanted then was to be an "AM" and not a "WAS".

The first New Year after I was home, we all went as usual to the New Year's Eve party in the village hall. I was very anxious about going, knowing that I wouldn't recognize anyone, that I'd struggle to keep with Ed and/or the family and that lots of people would say happy "Hellos!" to me and greet me as the friend I used to be. I still very much wanted to be their friend but that is very hard when I don't know anything about either of us anymore. One of my kind friends brought name badges for everyone to wear. The name alone didn't help me very much, but it announced my difficulties to everyone and I did get lots of hugs!

Sadly though, I felt that I was getting hugs for who I had been, and that I didn't actually deserve them for being who I am now. These people are giving me their side of friendship now unknown to me, they are kind and trying to understand and reassure me by reminding me of all the great times together but I feel completely separated from their happiness with no sense of belonging. They all seem pleased to see me, but I do not want to be this "me" any more, the one who doesn't know them, who lets them down and can't be their friend any more. As well as the prosopagnosia, I have 30 years of complete memory loss and great difficulty laying down new memories now, all of which reduces my confidence with every social interaction. Lots of people know lots of things about the person I was. Nobody knows very much about the person that I am now, least of all me.

Bonnie-Kate, the neuropsychologist, knew of a specialist neuro-rehabilitation centre and felt that I might benefit from having their type of support to help me to manage my difficulties in a more structured way. I was referred to their service and was assessed to see if they felt able to support me, and in what ways. My main difficulties were reported as having anxiety impacting on activities of daily living, and prosopagnosia, with difficulties appreciating the identity of other people. They reported decreased semantic memory, social inference difficulties and mood disturbance including anxiety, low mood and low confidence, causing restrictions impacting on relationships with my husband, family and friends. They noted my problems detecting humour and sarcasm and also that I was struggling to accept my loss of my work role as a nurse.

Barbara's comments: When Claire came for her one-day assessment at the Oliver Zangwill Centre, we found that her main problems were low confidence, anxiety, depression, poor facial recognition and organisational difficulties. She also had memory problems. Although she struggled to remember things from her past and found it hard to remember ongoing events or to learn new information, she was not severely amnesic and a few things stayed in her memory well. She has always remembered Bonnie-Kate, for example, and she has never forgotten that she had a visitors book while in hospital. Her preliminary assessment report from the centre can be seen in Appendix 1. We hope this will give a clear picture of the goals Claire and the team at the OZC were hoping to achieve as a result of her rehabilitation.

Note

1 Advanced Level Examinations are taken by British students at age 18 after completing GCSEs.

Chapter 9

The Red Group

Learning to belong to my own life

I was offered an intensive programme at the centre, four days a week for 24 weeks, to help me to develop greater awareness of my strengths and difficulties and to learn new ways of managing them more effectively. They felt that I would be able to benefit from their therapy and I consider myself very lucky to have been given this chance. They noted that my goals were to be able to return to work, to have a party where nobody needed to wear name labels, and to rediscover my own identity. Their assessment report ends by saying that "Claire and her family require an interdisciplinary team approach to maximize activity and participation in home, family, social and work domains. The interacting difficulties with cognitive functions, emotion regulation, and social processing present a barrier to achieving goals at present. The resulting frustration, anxiety, depression and loss of identity exacerbate her difficulties. Therefore the programme should include cognitive behavioural therapy to help with anxiety in particular, training in compensatory strategies for her cognitive and social impairments, and support for emotional adjustment, organised towards achieving specific functional goals. She is keen to learn about her condition, and to work with her family to learn how to re-establish herself and her identity. Her husband is keen to work with the therapy team and Claire has asked for help to improve their relationship. We will visit the family home to provide preliminary feedback and information to her children. We are keen to proceed with further rehabilitation as soon as possible."

I arrived for my time at the centre rather anxious about what might happen, and whether I would be able to manage all the tests properly and to be able to get better. They explained to me that their aims were for me to understand the consequences of my brain injury, to maximize my levels of independent functioning and to support me to adjust to my changed circumstances. I was scared of not re-finding "me" but saw this as my best chance. I needed to make sure that I did everything properly, to the best of my ability, to allow myself the best chance of recovering. The staff were understanding and caring throughout and I had confidence that my difficulties were understood and were normal and expected for my condition. They assessed and discussed these with me and goals were set for ways towards managing them. I had personal sessions to support me individually and group sessions with other clients. In these group sessions I felt helped to assess, accept and come to terms with my problems as they weren't just understood, but shared by the others. This helped me to feel very secure and I missed being there on my days off.

Near the beginning of the programme I was asked about day-to-day difficulties and I requested that people wear name badges as I was finding it very difficult to remember who anyone was. They understood and did this very quickly for me, which really helped. But it didn't tell me any more than a name, and at any moment I had no idea if I was interacting with one of the other clients or members of staff or somebody else passing through the centre. I asked again if they would distinguish staff and clients for me as I was finding it very difficult to know how to react to everyone appropriately. I was in a group of four clients; we all started our rehabilitation together. We were given red name badges—so we became the "Red Group". We immediately bonded and were able to share the experience of rehabilitation in a very supportive, together way. And I knew who they were!

The staff identified goals for me to reach during my time with them, including:

- to understand about brain injury;
- to be able to identify nine people;
- to re-familiarise myself with memories of significant family events;
- to reduce my anxiety and increase my levels of confidence such that I am able to engage in identified activities;
- to develop strategies to cope with communication consequences and the impact of these on my everyday communication with family and friends;
- for our family to communicate together to understand our shared and individual needs and systems to support each other;
- to develop a system allowing me to plan and organize my time and complete 75% of all planned activities;
- to be able to take photographs, to label them and to attend my photo scrapbooking group on a regular basis;

- to identify whether I can return to my job nursing (or something similar) and have a written vocational action plan for 6–12 months following completion of the rehabilitation programme.

The programme began, four days a week for six months, working towards "am" and away from "was". It included two parts, initially the Intensive Phase for three months followed by an Integration Phase. We worked with appropriate therapists for all our own personal individual needs in separate sessions throughout the day and we had regular group sessions when the four of us worked together with a therapist to learn about general, common difficulties. We worked together to discover some good ways to help ourselves and each other. We four were all very anxious when we arrived but soon formed a strong group bond and were very able to support and care about each other's differing needs. We had all had different reasons for our brain problems, resulting in different difficulties.

We had group sessions to give us information about brain injury generally and these allowed us very much to appreciate and understand our own problems and also each other's problems. My notes from that time say "sense-making sessions, and in 12 weeks we should be experts in our own brains and the consequential changes in our behaviour". UBI (Understanding Brain Injury) group sessions helped us to understand and to focus on the ways we do manage; it also helped us to keep sight of the positive ways we manage to help ourselves. We had Cognitive Group Sessions to appreciate all manner of invisible difficulties in everyday life, understanding the concept that the computer, or the controlling part of the brain, is the cognitive side. It is this part which helps us to operate effectively. It houses memory skills, co-ordination, executive functioning, speech and language, intelligence and concentration. Also common sense, visual perspective, fatigue and identity.

We had Psychological Support Group sessions together, forming goals to become supportive to each other. We needed to work together to achieve our chosen goals and we planned to make these sessions our times for thinking good things and trying to be generally positive. One day we chose to discuss voice intonations and changed pronunciations of things to give altered meanings. I learnt a lot from this session, and we all had a good laugh! Seems like we were in a very good mood—which we were all the time during our sessions as it felt so supportive and relaxing to be there together. We had Leisure Group outings which we organised together, all supporting each other to have separate responsibilities towards making the outings successful. Ensuring that we recognized each other's difficulties in meeting these responsibilities helped the event go well for each of us. We enjoyed a lovely walk around the town centre one day and I have some good photos to prompt my already lost memories of a really great day. We went swimming together one day as well—no photos, I promise!

We did Strategy Application group sessions together to identify our different skills and any difficulties with these. We also had to find strategies for management together. Each meeting we appointed a chair person to run the meeting and a secretary to take notes, print the notes and supply them to each of us to keep. At the end of each meeting we had feedback time to evaluate if our aims had been achieved, determine what had gone well and what we would do differently next time. We also compiled a newsletter, and we were asked to document how we felt we had personally contributed to it.

As well as our valuable group sessions, we all had individual sessions. I was given considerable support regarding my Occupational Health situation. I was helped to attend appointments to discuss whether or not I might be able to return to work, on what timescale and in what capacity. I was helped to prepare myself by taking various pieces of information with me, given ideas of how to say things, how to explain my goals to them and how I am working on achieving them. It was suggested that I use a tape-recording machine and have a period of relaxation time planned for myself before the appointment. I was encouraged to ask for a summary of the points of action and to confirm that the clinic staff were happy to work with the Occupational Health staff to support me in my return to work, if they would like to use this offer of help. The subsequent communication made me feel that this preparation helped the eventual decision-making through having a shared breadth of understanding.

The whole experience of being a "client" (that felt pretty strange) at the Oliver Zangwill Centre was hugely positive for me. It felt so different just being in an environment where my difficulties were expected and understood. I felt able to relax and to learn new strategies for managing my difficulties much better. It also helped very much being in a group environment and we gave each other a great deal of support, encouragement and great friendship. Friends—I know the staff weren't officially our friends but that is just how it felt—they noticed our tiny steps forward and valued them so well in very reassuring ways. We had many treasured moments when new understanding was shared.

We had useful teaching sessions where everything was explained clearly and our understanding was checked and we were supported by important things being gone over again when we needed this. The whole sense of being known to misunderstand and forget things allowed us to feel safe and reassured when we did misunderstand and forget, so we were, at all times, supported to manage better. For me, it helped hugely to have words, ideas, thoughts and strategies written down and that gave me the security of retaining memories when outside the Centre. The staff gave us printed information about our teaching sessions. I made many notes and I have gone back to these on many occasions to step on stones and save paddling through the river. In the world outside the Centre, people have little or no understanding of our difficulties and this gives them an expectation of our reactions and behaviour which they sometimes respond to in rather discomforting ways. I have had said to me "You never listen", "You just weren't listening", "I told you yesterday!", as well as the "Oh for god's sake", when I take a big deep breath. But I have strategies now! And I have them written down, and I know how to use them, when I remember them! (or even remember where I've put them). But I've made lists!

The friendship I made with the people in the Red Group during our time at the Centre together has been a very valuable continuation of sharing social times together with others who actually understand, care and share and with whom we can relax and feel allowed to be a bit "daft" at times! "Forgetful" is a whole step forward from feeling judged as being deliberately thoughtless.

Bonnie-Kate once said to me, "Claire, I've been with you since day one . . ." With you! That said it all and I was very happy and fortunate that she continued to visit me and support me as part of my programme at the Centre. I was given real support by her depth of understanding and caring. At the time of my illness our children were eight, ten, thirteen and fifteen years old and my poor husband was still a teenager at heart. The stability of their vulnerable, teenage years has been very severely affected by my confusion. Bonnie-Kate has been with me throughout all our difficulties, she understood my family relationship muddles and was always able to comfort and reassure me. I felt that she knew "me" and was able to understand and give me the capability of sorting things out in a better way for them and for me. She never took sides but was always able to show me the misunderstandings which led to our emotional distress. She set up experiments to test my negative thoughts and then to look for the evidence of what actually happened, for example when one of my annoyed teenagers barks at me "How would you know?".

The letters she sent home to me after each appointment are still very valuable to me and I have filed them carefully to re-read them whenever I have wanted to. For example "It can take a bit of practice to learn from these situations but we will persevere and get there!" "Together we can get you into the practice of stopping and thinking in a more balanced way to help control your anxiety and help build your confidence." "We can work together on this and bring about change." "WE" That's how it always felt—that she has been there with "me". Having the written word gave me real security and belief that her advice was safe and confidence that she had real belief that I could be a "me". She always reported when I had managed situations better—saying how good it was to hear that I have coped better with situations which have upset me in the past, saying that "we" can continue to increase my confidence and help me to feel more like "myself". The whole essence of "we" and "together we can" gave me a real strong feeling of being understood, of sharing and belonging to my own life.

Just writing this now about Bonnie-Kate is helping me to remember just how valuable her friendship and support has been to me over many years. I still use every bit of her advice to remind me how to manage my new life and try my best to believe that I am still myself.

Eighteen months after my initial illness I had another tonic-clonic seizure and needed a repeat brain scan. The consultant looked at it and said "I'm surprised you can put your own socks on." Bonnie-Kate never had to teach me this but I certainly feel that if she ever had to, that I'd be wearing knee highs by now!

I had always had superb help from my rehabilitation and I understood their strategies and the reasoning involved, but in the reality of home life I was often unable to think straight and remember their advice. I had to cope with my own obtuse ways of reasoning and much frustration. It was a terrible stage not only for me but for all my family as well, as much as they tried to help me. I know I reacted in ways they couldn't possibly understand and I know it was very upsetting for them.

I used all my learned strategies to help my long and short term memory problems as much as I possibly could: lists, lists and more lists and plenty of written instructions and plans, but the short term memory loss caused continuous difficulties with huge emotional upset regarding my social interactions in particular. My family did try to have patience and caring and were very understanding and tolerant whenever they could be. I know that life was difficult and distressing for them. As much as I tried to write everything down to feel some sense of security to manage things properly, I often forgot that, or where I had written it, and other complications in life had taken over.

I was receiving the help and support from all the staff at the Oliver Zangwill Centre but still struggling with my own complicated ideas when one day everything changed! Barbara came to give a talk at one of our group sessions and said these words which made me take a big deep breath and have the realisation about a huge misunderstanding I was making: "Rehabilitation is not synonymous with recovery." It may sound just like other jargon but those words turned a huge corner for me. I became able to understand that I shouldn't be expecting to recover. I was being given rehabilitation by utilising fantastic advice and support to help me move forward in accepting and managing the change to my life. And I was able to say to myself "One life, live it." The programme at the Oliver Zangwill Centre has helped me to learn strategies to do this. They can't do it for me. No one can mend my brain. Rehabilitation is not synonymous with recovery and recovery as a concept falls woefully short of the mark, but rehabilitation is giving me a second chance.

I then felt much more able to move forward in my life and continue to make the best of it without my constant feelings of guilt and that I am letting everyone down by not being "better".

Cognitive rehabilitation for me involved trying to learn how to recognize familiar faces and I was supported to try various methods to help me, particularly mnemonics which helped me to connect an identity of particular people to understand a bit more about them but I was not able to recognize them from the photos or face-to-face either. I said in Chapter 8 that I have a friend with long blonde curly hair and my mnemonic for her is "Golden Drop" as that is the name of the lane that she lives on. I am familiar with going down Golden Drop and visualizing the lane and her house enables me to have some memories of who she is, which is great, but I sadly cannot recognize her face-to-face despite her lovely curls.

The staff worked long and hard with me to help me use compensatory strategies to try and grasp identity memories about other people. I have found a few people's voices trigger connections for me, and although I usually don't have the confidence to believe myself, I regularly end up needing to kick myself when they tell me who they are before I've had the chance to say "hello", and their name! Greeting somebody by name is something taken for granted, as a special social way to greet people, the same is true of saying "hiya". It says so many hidden things—"I know you!", "I like you!", "I'm pleased to see you!". These social greetings are completely lost to me and although I value all my compensatory strategies, "Sorry, who are you?" just isn't quite the same.

Visual clues of people's identity were made and recorded at length which has been great and I have referred back to these words to remind myself of visual triggers which I may use to help me identify people, such *as moustache, hairstyle, particular glasses, height etc.—the problem with this is that these change! So do the places where I see people, and as lovely as it is to be hugged by the person as I arrive at their front door, knowing who I am visiting, it's a complete shock if they do it to me in the supermarket, and they happily tell me their name thinking that I'll then know them.*

Names and identities linking together are very difficult for me and a name on its own is an empty soul. People are so happy to be saying who they are, but sadly "Pat!", "Linda!", "Louise!" reminds me that these are names I've heard of, or even that I once knew people with these names; but I absolutely do not know them anymore. As well as the face-to-face identity difficulties I have, there are also phone calls from people I am meant to know, group conversations about people I used to know, or somebody just asking me about somebody else.

I was given speech and language therapy to help me with word-finding, turn-taking and non-verbal communication, particularly teasing. I was taught how to establish the intent of somebody's interaction by trying to assess or read their body language, facial expressions, positioning and tone of voice. I was told to not just take everything said to me literally. This included comments like "Get a life!", "How would you know?", "You never listen!".

I also had cognitive behaviour therapy at the OZC to help reduce my anxiety and understand the relationship between thoughts, feelings and behaviour. This allowed me to feel more confident about myself, particularly within the family. Although I still struggled to do things differently, I could understand the benefit of thinking and acting in more flexible ways. I was encouraged to make notes on a record sheet of differing incidents and to monitor and assess what happened, whether I coped well, or not so well, and which items I may have addressed differently. This helped me to identify communication misunderstandings and better ways to cope with these in my everyday life. Thinking things through and making notes really helped me then, and although it took time and many big deep breaths, it made me feel more understanding and less antagonized.

One of the long-term goals I had made at the centre was to complete a time line of stages in my life, so that I could feel more strength in belonging to my own life by having rather more understanding about it. I began by making a photo scrapbook of my times at the centre, which has formed a very important part of my memory bank of my times there. Before my illness, I had been happily doing photo scrapbooking and the whole concept of making memories very visible and protected was very reassuring to me then. I had been doing this with the support of Creative Memories, a company from which we bought equipment, using lots of their advice and planning ideas. Sadly Creative Memories has now closed, but their methods and equipment are still with me. I was used to adding the written word to the pages to give background information, and of course, names of people! I've written whose birthday it was! I'd had a long period of time not feeling confident to do this anymore so when I was asked "Claire, what is your leisure activity?" I felt very ready to have support to regain it.

The album I made with lots of help and encouragement has photos of the Red Group, our leisure outings, our evening meals out together and happy times spent when I was doing my voluntary placements during the Integration Phase (I talk about this in a minute). It was so positive for me to get back to making real visual memories that I have subsequently started to make a rather complicated album as my time line.

The first part of the rehabilitation programme was called the Intensive Phase and the second part was called the Integration Phase. We were integrating back into our own lives and were helped to face our difficulties and be supported to step out into the big wide world more generally with increasing confidence. We were each given two days a week doing voluntary work in placements chosen either by the staff or by us. The staff took great care to enrol each of us to undertake valuable voluntary work which suited each of us personally and which would provide understanding and support for our difficulties.

I was given a day a week helping in a National Trust Park and another day a week in a special school. At the National Trust site I helped the Education Team, who had school groups and other visitors learning about nature. I loved doing collages and pictures using twigs and leaves with the children and, as for the pond dipping—who was going to be the first to catch a newt—that was very exciting! I was really able to relax and it felt very positive and caring to be able to help the children both learn and have fun—and they didn't expect me to know them from one minute to the next!

In my other voluntary day, I was able to choose for myself and I was accepted in our local special school where I helped with one of their classes which had a number of pupils in wheelchairs. Just another pair of hands could enable them to go out into the town or down to the park for part of their day. It felt really good to be able to help other people again and although I didn't always know just who were the staff, and who were the pupils, I was able to feel secure and helpful pushing one wheelchair within a group and happily reacting as appropriately as I could to each individual who made contact with me. It was a very positive experience for all of us to go out of the school for a short time. Sometimes we had tea and cakes or ice-creams down by the river feeding the ducks. It was relaxing and supportive for the pupils and this made me feel better, being able to improve their lives for a short time. The children's appreciation of my prosopagnosia was not quite so easy in the special school as I had been their school nurse prior to my illness and I would have known many of them very well by name and been very understanding of their difficulties. Even so, the words of their headmaster gave me much reassurance when I was anxious about this—"Claire, you belong here." Doing the voluntary work in the Integration Phase was very positive for me and gave me much more self-confidence about things I can manage, and it enabled me to positively use the strategies I had learned about in the Intensive Phase to be able to support myself better.

The other two days a week in the Integration Phase were spent at the Oliver Zangwill Centre continuing with group and individual sessions. We worked at trying to improve my general self-confidence, specifically at home, and I used planned strategies to try things out. I had some very positive feedback from my own children. "You're much better than you were before." We had used strategies involving eye contact, tone of voice, volume of voice, body language and gesture. When I deliberately tried to make more eye contact with my children, the quality of our interactions really improved and this made each of us feel better.

I had been helped to make lists to improve my general memory systems, particularly using a Filofax and not just thousands of pieces of scrap paper to try and organize my life whilst in the Intensive Phase. This progressed into supporting me to manage time restrictions better and employing general organizational skills using a to-do list. It was noted in the Integration Phase that I was becoming more able to consider how to improve things for myself by having a structured way of recording things.

It was also noted that at times I impulsively write down things in random places when anxious and I was encouraged to use a STOP THINK[1] strategy, which has really worked. I need to PAUSE (stop), REFLECT (consider what I need to write down), SELECT (decide where is the best place to write this information so that I will able to find it again) and RECORD (write it down).

I'm happy to say that my Outcome Report from the centre notes that my voluntary work placements have been a valuable part of my rehabilitation, that they gave me opportunities to identify, implement and evaluate strategies within supportive environments.

Sadly though, it was during this time that I was assessed by the Occupational Health team and advised that they would be retiring me on ill-health grounds, as it was not possible to re-deploy me within their Trust. Although this broke my heart, I was able to understand that my memory problems and prosopagnosia would prevent me from acting safely and to preserve everyone's best interest it was better for someone else to be doing my job. I felt a complete failure but I knew I would be an actual failure if I were to be trusted with the title of "nurse" again. It just wasn't to be and I told myself that I would make a much better effort at being mum, wife, friend, daughter, sister, auntie etc. and look after others in a voluntary placement to allow me to feel of some value to the world from a position of safety.

Barbara's comment: See Appendix 2 for further information on how the OZC team helped Claire prepare for her meeting with the Occupational Health board.

When I finished the programme at the Centre, I went through a low period. I did not appreciate it at the time but have understood since that I was having a normal experience following rehabilitation: the "post-re-hab slump". I had come so far with all the advice and support that I had started to struggle to accept or even acknowledge my limitations. I had forgotten that I wasn't the person I used to be and I expected myself to manage life in my old routine ways. I completely misjudged my own abilities to cope. Having been cared about and supported by the rehabilitation team and known to have difficulties, I then found myself out in the big wide world feeling judged against the person I used to be, the person they think I was appearing to be and the person they wished me to be now. But it wasn't "me" and, in the attempt to feel normal, I had become increasingly able to appear to be "normal" and then judged as if I were normal. The judgement felt threatening and unfair. It was like having to go back to school again but with no satchel full of books, no equipment and no information. My uniform was tattered and my hair a mess, where my desk was I just had to guess. All the other pupils are busy, having direction. I panic and feel I have no connection. I think most of the judgement was within myself and my own sense of loss but I did feel very much that my efforts at appearing normal and trying to react normally were never understood. There was no concept of just how difficult this was for me. Almost every moment of life involves memories and understanding to act appropriately and all circumstances involved are ever changing by the second. To appear normal involves thinking. Thinking is a chaotic spin of thoughts for me which is very tiring and I am not quick enough to match up to the expectations of real life any more. I had to realise what I could and could not manage and be more honest with myself as to how much I should attempt to do. I think at that time I had emotional exhaustion, which is different to how I imagine depression. Thinking and caring was wearing me out and not having the right person to speak to about it was sad. Having had a good sense of direction in life before, I knew I just had to get on with it, make the best of it and try not to involve other people having to worry about it. Carrying on with the voluntary work I started as part of my programme helped me to get over the post-rehab slump and see a continuation of the improvement ahead of me.

Barbara's notes: The Red Group was particularly supportive and all four people bonded well and formed strong friendships. Once Claire started the programme at the Oliver Zangwill Centre much of the work on reducing her anxiety and improving her self confidence was directed by Fergus Gracey (see Chapter 4). The Integration Phase is an important part of the comprehensive rehabilitation programme as it gradually re-introduces clients to everyday life again while still providing support and structure from staff members at the Centre.

Note

1 This is described in Chapter 12.

Chapter 10

A face is not a person

Facial recognition was something I know I was previously very good at, and my husband now tells me just how much he relied on me to know who people were. But now, for me, a face could be anybody. Facial expressions are what I try to use to ascertain whether the person is an individual supposedly known to me. Humans have a multitude of facial expressions which change extremely quickly, and body language and mannerisms can say a lot about what they are thinking. We can't read people's minds but that is almost what I'm trying to do each time I look at a face. What I want, and need to know very quickly, is whether they know me? And then, how well? And in what circumstances do we share parts of our lives together? I need a lot of reliable information in those few immediate seconds, from seeing the face, and very specifically from making eye contact, to ensure that I respond appropriately to them.

One day a close friend of mine took me to a taster day at one of our local health clubs. I wasn't really planning to join one but I went along hoping to enjoy some more times together and make new memories in our friendship. We walked through the door and it just felt like home! It was familiar! I was engulfed with a real rush of warmth the instant they showed us the swimming pool, which had a real emotional connection for me. I can't remember now if I realised myself or if Carolyn reminded me that this was where my children had learned to swim. I could almost feel them there when we saw the baby pool. I felt so connected to it that this was definitely for me. I went initially only with my friend and she stayed with me while we tried different activities together as, at that time, I was struggling to get out and about on my own and kept losing my way. But I am loads better than the day when one of my neighbours had to show me the way when I was only two doors from home, in a big panic marching up and down the pavement!

I had started to drive again when we went to the health club and began to have confidence to go on my own (my way! OK a bit longer but, at least, I got there). Where I had left my car when I was looking for it later, well nobody knows! I must have found it eventually.

One day I gathered my confidence and tried aqua aerobics, an exercise class to music in the pool. At the end of the class, the trainer came up to me and said "I could see by your face that you've found the right thing for you" and how right she was. I had a real sense of belonging to that place and then, being in the pool and leaping up and down to known old music was a real pleasure for me. There is nothing like a bit of exercise to make you feel better. I could imagine my two eldest there in the baby pool, learning to swim and that happiness stays with me. It's a memory!

I have gradually made some new friends at this class but, as there are 20 ladies at each one, and all club members can choose to attend as many as we like out of the eight sessions a week, it is a real mixture (muddle) of just who will be there. I try to attend three and sometimes four sessions a week and, doing so, may come into contact with 60 to 80 other ladies. Some attend in groups, some with friends but most, like me, come along on their own. Everyone is very friendly and there is plenty of moving around each other and in the changing rooms and coffee lounge afterwards, such that, for me, the sea of unknown faces is constantly changing. Having needed to retire early, I am about 15–20 years younger than most of the others, which means that I can jump higher, move more quickly and be in serious danger of splashing their hair! I don't make easy eye contact and I rush off at the end so I don't barge into the wrong group of ladies having coffee afterwards. I expect I look a bit anxious from time to time, so the mums among them have attempted to be friendly and tried to look after me. I was very grateful for this, initially, but it has been awful just having no idea which of them have been so kind to me. Every time I go, there are 20 of us getting ready together and then getting into the water and finding our places. I haven't any idea who I spoke to a minute ago, five minutes ago, earlier on today or yesterday. Let alone all the other ladies who do only set times once a week and expect all the others to know them. Nowadays, I try to make eye contact quickly and say blandly "Fine thanks and how are you?" smiling in an encouraging way so that whether they know that I don't know them or not, I appear friendly and caring about them socially. It feels rather a false pretence of knowing them and can lead to conversations right out of my depth. But lots of happy time is spent with empty general chit chat. Although that isn't a chosen way for me to socialise, it has given me *confidence to be able to better judge how to make the best of these social situations and it has allowed me to feel included again. Also I can watch all the little ones learning to swim while I am desperately trying not to splash Rita or Joan! (who have made sure they've reminded me who they are). There is one lady with long dark curly hair, which I initially used to remind myself that she was Pat and very kind to me. I looked out for her to give me confidence to be correctly sociable and she looked out for me too. It made all the difference to have one special reminder of some security in caring and friendly Pat. This allowed me to feel able to tell her why I was being rather shy with huge social uncertainty. The decision to tell or not tell people about my difficulties is an area of uncertainty for me but Pat gave me confidence to do so. Now I arrive to some big grins and ladies not asking how I am but telling me who they are "Hello, Claire, I'm Lucy", or others with shy grins who probably can't believe that I don't know them, as I was there with them yesterday, after all. Pat understood that, although I smiled and chatted in the changing room, she needed to remind me again once we were in the pool, and again when we were back in the changing room again. Then she would make sure I had an arrange-ment to meet up for coffee afterwards and would look out for me. Bless her, her kindness has made all the difference for me. I stay and have coffee with them sometimes. As new friends, they don't know the "me" (who I don't know any more) and, sadly, I have found this rather easier than keeping up with all the old friends whose need to remind me has been very kind but which has been upsetting for me. However, my newer friends are becoming old friends now and suddenly having expectations of my behaviour, including memories, which is almost harder for them as they never had the chance of understanding quite what I have been through. Or why I can't remember. I have written notes in my friendship book to remind me about their needs and feelings but I don't have it with me at the pool, and, of course, I can't rely on clothing there either!*

In the chapter I wrote with Barbara in Life After Brain Injury: Sur-vivors' Stories, *I have written about one situation which happened there—"One day recently I'd been to my aqua-aerobics class where I enjoy exercising in the pool with a group of other ladies. We were all back in the changing room and I suddenly realised that one of them was looking at me. I caught her eye and tried to decide if she wanted to speak to me, or if I was expected to remember something, or know her? I glanced away to gain a second breath, and then looked back towards her to see if she was still making any social contact with me. I saw that she'd also looked away and was then making eye contact with me again. I was unsure if she knew me or not or whether she was going to say* anything, and she looked uncertain about whether she was going to or not. I began to feel rather uncertain about this person and worried that I possibly seemed aloof and unfriendly towards her as she was clearly trying to connect with me in some way, but just not being sure made me hope that she'd make the first social interaction so that I could respond if I needed to. We looked rather uncertainly at each other several times before somebody walked between us and I suddenly realised that it was a mirror! And I had been looking at me! No wonder she was looking so confused" (Wilson & Claire, 2013, p. 105).

The oddities of social behaviour! I think I used to understand the expectations of social contact amongst individuals. Although I feel confident that I still understand these, my parameters have had to change in the chaotic muddle of strangers who I live with and exist around. I think I have got used to reading much more into people's behaviour so that I have had to guard myself from feeling or seeming nosey. Because someone unknown may greet me unexpectedly in a public place (and this happens often now), I almost dread it happening and my reactions are on edge in the hope that I can protect myself from all the embarrassment and confusion; consequently, I am watching out much more. Passing too easily as "normal" makes it very difficult as people expect me to act as normal and make judgements regarding my behaviour as if there was nothing the matter with me.

OK, here it is: the first thing I see or hear is a person, somebody. A lot depends on where I am and who else I know who is around me, if anybody. My first need is to know if they are intending to make contact with me, and then decide carefully upon watching their reactions towards me. They may be a complete stranger who just happened to glance at me, and either ignored me or took a second to decide if they knew me, or if they liked my necklace. They may be someone who knows me by name and we have shared small parts of our lives together, maybe we both helped at cub scouts or our daughters went to ballet together or they could be a friend of my mother's or an old work mate. And now they are smiling at me! That feels nice but brings on a complete panic as I don't know the best way to react to them. I have become very practised at false friendship—almost pretending how pleased I am to see them before having any idea who they are. Being initially happy feels good but then the admission of not recognising them becomes harder to deal with emotionally. However, it allows those first few seconds of panic to pass. OK, we've said "Hello, how are you?" and the usual "Fine thanks" is done. Then comes the next bit—a barrage of questions about my life, all with heavy inference that they know things about it and are being sociable, friendly or caring by wanting to know more. But who are they? And how do they know so much about me? And what should I say? Is it more important at this moment that I don't know who they are, or that I don't know the answers to the questions they are asking about me? My confidence for social interactions depends on the circumstances of this meeting, whether I am expecting to meet up with anyone in particular or not and how many people are around. In addition, the reactions of each specific individual are often very difficult to read.

It all feels very awkward, I need to know if they know that I won't know them. How much do I need to ask or say? It is a few moments of complete uncertainty with many concerns flying about in the chaos of my brain—not to mention my shaking shoulders and my wobbly knees. Should I say "Please remind me who you are?" and hope that they won't feel that my happy greeting and near pretence of already knowing them will make them feel awkward and unsure. "What's your name?" is always there in desperate circumstances but I do try other ways first if the person doesn't seem to realise that I don't actually know them. Sometimes "How do we know each other?" or "Where did we meet" can be used but it all depends on the other person's reactions. Initially, there were many people who did not understand that I had no idea who they were but nowadays there are many more people who tell me very quickly their name. Over time I have learned to read their understanding of my difficulties beyond them telling me their name. Some people realise quickly that they need to give me a few more details regarding their identity and/ or how we know each other to jog some disconnected memories about them. Lots of odd bits of memories can be happily jogged in this way but I cannot access them with just a face and a name. I need to fit together some pieces of my jigsaw.

At the beginning I would say gently to people that I had no facial recognition in the hope that it would explain my difficulties to them but it either gave them the concept that I would know them if they gave me their name or they would say "Oh, yes, I never remember names either."

Some people continue to think that once they have told me their name, that should be all I need in order to know who they are. They can then get confused and even insulted if I have to ask them some more. "I'm sorry, Sally, please tell me which Sally you are." I know far too many Lindas and don't know where to start with people who say "I'm Linda". Different pieces of information evoke identity connections for different people, but very often I find that if somebody tells me where they live, and if I can visualise their home, that brings up fragments of information *about who they are and which Linda it is. To help me manage these times much better I have made myself the "A–Z Identity Book". It's a small address book, which fits in my handbag so I can have it with me at all times. I have put people's names and then instead of an address I've written how and why I know them. It's a few words which prompt my memory of their identity and I can refer to it quickly so that I can meet, speak to, or about, in a meaningful, social, understanding way. Having my A–Z Identity Book in my handbag has allowed me to piece together the fragments of information I have about each person I may meet if I know about the meeting in advance, but it cannot help me when I am suddenly hugged in the town centre or phoned unexpectedly.*

Barbara's comment: The A–Z Identity Book is Claire's most helpful aide memoire. She mentions it often and describes it in more detail in Chapter 11.

People generally behave appropriately to each other without having to make conscious decisions about who somebody is and the correct way to interact with them. Losing this ability has been socially very stressful. Many thoughts are read into our behaviour and whether they are appreciated and understood rightly or wrongly makes a significant difference to our ability to socialise correctly. Socialising correctly? That is an important issue. No one wants to ignore or not seem to care about meeting up with their family and friends, nor do they want to happily greet and hug the wrong person at the railway station. I used to know which boy to watch at the football match, which ones were mine at the swimming pool, which person I was sitting with when out having a coffee. Now, I do not see anything meaningful in their face and have to rely on their behaviour, facial expressions, eye contact, body language and general demeanour to help me feel confident to know their identity. They tend to think that once I seem to know them, at our next interaction only seconds later, that I will still know them and they expect me to behave as such. I manage a lot better one to one with people. As soon as others are around just keeping confident of one person's identity from one moment to the next is very stressful. When there are uniforms worn, it is hopeless and the visual impact of these just overwhelms any hopes of maintaining identity appreciation. I regularly rely on items of clothing to help. Name badges make all the difference and enable a much better hope for me to react and interact the right way with the right people. When I am in a social group I tend to glue myself to particular people that I feel secure to stay with. I very carefully note to myself a visual reminder to help me, usually an item of clothing, sometimes jewellery, hair styles even handbags or a visible mole will do.

I'm not planning to do this, but have had fun imagining badges for me to wear which would probably help me: "Where's your name badge?" or . . . "If you know me, please tell me who you are, and how we know each other?" even . . . "I'm guessing, please give me the chance!", "Claire somebody", "I don't know you, let alone me."

I have a great visual memory of one day noticing a chap wearing a T-shirt with this printed on it: "Sorry, but I left my name badge at home today." That gave me a good laugh and has stayed in my memory!

I have very few memories of my own life and those I can speak of are described as "my well rehearsed stories" like "I was born a nurse" or "It was better to get off at the bus at the bottom of the road and walk uphill than get off at the terminus when I had high heels on." These sayings do bring back some vague memories. The memories I am given by others feel as if they are speaking of the life of a stranger, almost like they are reading a book to me. Somebody, I am not sure who, woke up in hospital having survived encephalitis but not its consequences.

My happy memories are from the Red Group reunions, the User Group meetings, the Transylvania Trek (see Chapter 12 for more detail) and the "Wear a Name Label" party that we held at our house after I had finished rehabilitation.

Chapter 11

Strategies that have helped

Barbara has asked me to talk about my life now. I have come a long way since I kissed the cauliflower thinking it was Ed! Before I start with all the practical chaos, I just want to say that I am feeling much more secure about my life now as I am using many strategies to guard and record my memories.

I have rehabilitated well (not recovered). I am left with prosopagnosia, short- and long-term memory loss, risk of further fitting, reduced speed of thought and poor organisational abilities. I get tired easily and have regular headaches, am anxious most of the time with low self confidence. I am sensitive to sudden loud sounds, sudden unexpected movements and bright lights. I need to avoid situations with flashing lights or high pitch music to prevent me having another fit. I am lucky to have warning signals and the physical ability to alter the circumstances around me. I have anosmia (loss of sense of smell) but am very happy I can see the daffodils even if I can't smell them. And I have children at home who tell me when I have left the gas on! Taste wise, things are improving and I am managing to try and enjoy a few sweet things without them tasting metallic. A bit of lemon, mint or ginger can really help the chocolate be almost nice. I feel I must be mending some connections over time. I am usually quite stubborn, trying very hard to manage all my own expectations and hopes for myself without bothering others so as to hang on to some fragments of my own self-esteem. But I know that I am unsafe at times and have learned the hard way—as we all do. Life is not a dress rehearsal and I am trying to relearn about Claire Robertson from all the other people who know and understand much more about her than I do.

Let's visit a typical day for me. The alarm goes off. I awake on my side of the bed with the man I believe to be Ed. Then there's the school run—chaos for everyone! I have shared this palaver with all four of our kids and their friends over the years, but now that I can't recognise them or any of their friends or remember who needs to go where—it is all a bit of a scare. I feel very shy to ask my friends' children who they are, again, and where to take them, again, and it can be very embarrassing for my children to have Mum having to ask everyone again, including them! Even when they have told me, I can't remember a minute later and need to ask again. Over time I have learned to keep calm and try to be friendly, however confused and fed-up they get to be, but I very much want them to realise that I do care very much about them all individually, but through the years of "teenage rampage" it's been a very big learning curve for all of us.

OK, that's the school run done, I can go and do my exercise class. I have time now that I am not able to work. I've been to aqua aerobics, my serious prosopagnosia challenge, I get out into the car park and encounter other people parking and going in. They may or may not know me, speak to me, or wish to ignore me, I drive home, and whether I risk the same difficulties at Sainsbury's (the supermarket) is another question. Do I risk it? But I need to do the shopping, my family rely on me to manage this. Before I know it, I am being hugged in the fridge department by somebody very pleased to bump into me, and they seem to know me! Who can they be? I go to the till with the lady working there, who happily greets me like an old friend as well. I have learned to respond to this in a friendly way and keep packing the bags and reading labels rather than making eye contact with anyone else. I say "Bye" very certainly and escape to the car without looking at anybody, in case I get another "Hello Claire". I think I must look very worried to people, who seem to warm to me as if I'm a frightened child.

Home, where the post is on the doorstep and some of it is addressed to me. Who is it from? I try to assess the writing and the postmark and work out if it might be something I am expecting. I may open it up and find a name "Joe Bloggs". I don't recognise the postmark and the written piece is small and all scrunched up and becomes impossible for anyone else to read. But it says "Hi, Claire", as if someone is there, and the more I decipher, the harder it is to understand who has kindly sent me this card. My first visit is to my A–Z Identity Book, which will help me to realise who this is from. I look up their name, helpful if I can work out the surname but each page becomes a discovery in itself. It tells me which Linda it is from and how we know each other. I have a rush of sadness with lost memories but a warm secure feeling that our friendship is still building, Building! That says it all—the "wall of friendship" becomes stronger with every meaningful, understood contact. And the great thing about the written word is that I can keep it. It has a security of its own and I store it in the right section of my Friendship File. It feels as if our friendship is still intact and I can revisit it whenever I like, and, hopefully share it with Linda too.

Phone calls are nowhere near as easy as the written word. I still dread answering the phone and rarely use it for socialising if I can avoid it. The spoken word goes too quickly for me. I can't remember it in time to allow me to appreciate what is being said. E-mails and phone texts are not so easy to store and feel secure about. Although I know that printing off a computer is expensive and not the best thing for the environment, I find myself using the printer and storing words in a desperate attempt to keep control of my own understanding of what has happened in my life and relevant aspects of other people's lives. Texts get scribbled and stored, in another "waste" of paper, but they feel like a more secure way of accessing parts of my memory. How to get somewhere to share life seemed to be so easy and taken for granted before I lost my memories and confidence in my ability to navigate myself. Now that I have been able to re-use the written directions over and over again, I use this less and less now and find myself following my nose and sense of direction. My visual memories of these written words and maps have made all the difference. I have made myself a "Present File", recording who has kindly given me which gifts, as I felt heartbroken knowing that I have some lovely items but no idea which kind person chose them for me. Choosing presents and using them is all part of the fabric of friendship and love—it also shows that we choose to care about that person's needs and feelings by giving them lovely things. I have felt much more secure about my gratitude now that I am making written records. I can even use the right mug when my mother-in-law comes round for tea! And wear that lovely top she always reminds me that we chose together. Caring needs protecting and, in order to feel caring towards others, I need to store many memories to ensure that I react to them correctly. I have had many different files and lists. One day I came across an A4 arch file with photos of alphabetti spaghetti all over it, with the letters spelling "Brain Food". It was for me! In it, I keep my own important information files and documents, which I need to keep safe in order to continue to cope with being me.

Writing to people isn't easy, as I need to evoke my own thoughts and feelings in order to make meaning out of what I am writing about. It's like coming into a random chapter in a book you've never read. You open the page, expect to know what's happened, what's happening and guess where it's all going! I gather together all my friendship files and pieces of writing I've stored and these help me to feel that I am more able to write *to this person. Thank goodness for pen and paper, and how fortunate I am to be able to see.*

Over ten years of troubles I have come a long way with managing my difficulties as best I can without being able to recognise people by their faces. I am going to try to explain how things have improved.

The following are the strategies and devices I use now.

Current memory system:

- *Filofax—excellent resource but in a big muddle*
- *Daily To Do Diary—now using the following method:*
  - *As and when*
  - *If ever*
  - *To do*
- *White board on fridge*
- *Family diary*
- *Notebook in camera case to make notes*
- *A–Z identity jig—the best thing ever!*
- *Friendship Book and Friendship File, a great new device but well behind where I want it to be*
- *SenseCam work and diary writing—very helpful*
- *Jobs to do list, shopping lists and reminders*
- *More organised boxes with named files*
- *New photo organisation box—in chaos*
- *Book of written directions*
- *Files for paperwork that needs doing, labelled to remind me what to do with them*
- *Recipes that have worked notebook*
- *Meal planning and shopping lists*
- *Notepaper by phone.*

And now I have scribbled all this lot, I need to re-read all my rehabilitation advice and use it again to get even better organised.

Chapter 12

Can you believe your eyes?

Sight difficulties following encephalitis

Can you believe your eyes? Yes, my eyes are telling me the truth but my brain is not believing it. The damaged areas of my brain cannot process all the messages from my eyesight all the time so that I misunderstand what I am seeing in awkward ways. My eyes are not telling lies, I just don't get the gist of some of the messages they are trying very hard to give me. I have fairly good eyesight when I am wearing my glasses but I do have a degree of astigmatism. One optician told me he knew what my prescription would be just by looking at me. My main problem regarding vision is people. Prosopagnosia is a long word meaning stranger—I don't recognise faces, appreciate identity, age, race or gender. Mirrors give me a real fright.

Also problematic are other live creatures—animals, birds, our own pets and also models of live creatures, which regularly make me jump out of my skin and gives anyone around me a good laugh. Less problematic but still awkward in daily life is that I don't recognise some items around the house or remember how to use them, or where we keep them. I don't recognise the cupboards and drawers and frequently have to refer to the written word to find and use things. I don't know which items of clothing are mine or which belong to each of the others.

Ed commented on Claire's problem with animals, saying "She once held out to me in her hands, a hornet and said 'Look at this' and I went 'AAH, it's a hornet'; she didn't seem fearful, but she didn't know what it was." He also mentioned that soon after Claire came out of hospital, "One of the early things she said to me when we were driving past a field of sheep and she said to me 'What are those?' and I said 'they're sheep.' And she said 'Do they make wool?' I said 'Yes' and she said 'That seems completely wrong.' Again there was a disconnect between the sheep idea and what she knew in her mind sheep do. It was really interesting. She said.

'I can't join those things up. I know sheep make wool and I know those things are sheep and they are hairy and woolly' but she couldn't believe, her brain wouldn't believe that fact that her mind was telling her."

I try to focus on what I have got, which is sight. I feel lucky to have this and to be able to use it to support me to value and enjoy life and to make new me.

Barbara's comments: I have observed people, who should know better, show how basic their misunderstanding of Claire's difficulties is. For example, I recently introduced someone from a charity to Claire. She had met him before but of course did not recognise him. I was about to remind her who he was and where she had met him before when he said, very confidently, "Oh, Claire knows me." Claire was confused as she certainly did not recognise him.

The mnemonics Claire mentioned, which she used to help her try to identify and remember people (and are described in Chapter 8), can be valuable ways to learn more quickly and efficiently. Mnemonics are systems that enable us to remember things more easily. Most of us use mnemonics occasionally. For example, in the UK and the USA most people use a rhyme to remember how many days there are in each month. In other parts of the world knuckles and dips on the hand are used (knuckles represent long months and the dips between them represent short months). Still other countries use suffixes and prefixes to remember the long and the short months. Every country using our calendar system has a mnemonic for remembering months of different lengths. Visual mnemonics can be defined as "remembering by pictures". These may be mental images or actual pictures. Claire used these successfully to some extent: thus she could remember that the neighbour with the golden curls lived on Golden Drop Lane but this did not help her recognise the face of the neighbour. Compensatory procedures are usually more successful than mnemonics and Claire does, indeed, compensate up to a point. She knows that Ed wears a shark tooth locket and this enables her to recognise Ed. She can frequently pick out a photo of herself by recognising a necklace she wears or, if she is smiling in the photograph, she notices her false tooth. Her Identity Book she describes is also, of course, a compensatory procedure.

One of Claire's goals was to have a party where the guests did not have to wear name badges. This was to be the "No Name Label Party". As the time approached to have this party, however, Claire realised that she would not manage if people did not wear name badges so she switched to calling it a "Wear a Name Label Party". I attended this party held at Claire's home and it was a great success. Claire is very socially skilled;

despite her doubts she is a good friend to many people and she was a very good hostess at her party.

Claire also mentioned the "Stop Think" strategy. This comes from the Goal Management Framework (GMF). Based on the work of Duncan (1986) and Robertson (1996), the GMF is a five-step problem-solving strategy: (1) stop and think, (2) define the main task, (3) list the steps, (4) learn the steps (if necessary) and put them into action, and (5) monitor the situation. This is a fundamental part of the rehabilitation offered at the OZC for people with planning and organisational problems.

Behavioural experiments, also mentioned by Claire, derive from Cognitive Behaviour Therapy. They are designed to test out the validity of a person's beliefs. (Bennett-Levy *et al.*, 2004). So, for example, Claire felt she could not be a good friend as she did not recognise people and could not remember what she and her friends had in common. She thought that without her face recognition and autobiographical memories her friends would think her rude. She had started the Friendship Book after discussions with Bonnie-Kate and her pre illness interest in making scrapbooks. Bonnie-Kate and Claire made a plan to visit a friend and work on the Friendship Book together. Claire realised that she was able to talk about past times with her friend and they enjoyed working together on the book (see Figures 12.1 and 12.2). Her reflections on this were along the lines

Figure 12.1   One of Claire's collages, which she made to keep her treasured memories safe.

Figure 12.2 Claire's collage of a special trip to York.

of "we can still have our special friendship despite my difficulties". For a while Claire was reassured about her ability to be a friend but in 2013, when preparing for this book, she was, once again, doubtful about this.

Chapter 13

"Metallic not sour" and pieces of the jigsaw

Right from being discharged home I received regular letters from the Encephalitis Society. For a long period of time I felt very afraid of looking at any of this correspondence, or speaking to anyone about it. I was already struggling to help myself with the many pieces of advice and support I was already lucky to have. I could not quite cope with the possibility of putting another angle on it and stopping my good feelings of going forwards.

It was more than two or three years later that I felt able to access some of their information and I started to look at some of this. It was interesting and informative and gave me more confidence and security that the way I was feeling was to be expected and was normal given what had happened to me. The logo of the Encephalitis Society shows two pieces of life's jigsaw fitting back together and I am not sure if it was through this, or that I read something somewhere, that made me visualise my own jigsaw of life, and say to myself that the jigsaw of my life had fallen off the top shelf and I was desperately trying to pick up the pieces and fit it back together.

It was heartbreaking but I eventually had to accept that I was not going to be able to return to work, to be a nurse, so I felt I was never going to be me. After much testing and explanation I was given ill-health retirement and this gave me much more drive to continue with the voluntary work that I was already doing, and to fit some more in too. I used all my organisational strategies learned at the Centre but, once more, took on too much and did not allow for my own organisational difficulties and poor time management. So I was continually forgetting that thinking takes so much longer now and making decisions is a nightmare. I lived a life insistent on managing, using very strict rules for myself while being unrealistic about just how much I could manage. A large part of my time is taken up decision making, trying to evaluate all possible ifs and buts

*of any of my actions. The rest of my time is spent rushing and doing it
wrong.*

*As I began to gain back my confidence to travel by public transport
again, I started to attend open meetings run by the Encephalitis Society
(www.encephalitis.info). I was interested to see if they had any new ideas
about how I might manage things better. Their meetings were very informative and everyone was made to feel very welcome and cared about. At
one meeting there was a request for people to join a trek to Transylvania. We were asked to put our hands up. I sneaked my hand up rather
uncertainly and another person not far away did the same. We looked at
each other and made our own mental note to get together. We wondered
how we would manage to trek Transylvania but we were both going to do
it. She asked me what my main problem was, and when I said prosopagnosia—she said so was hers! We made an instant friendship and have
shared our difficulties together and given each other much understanding
and support, which has been really wonderful. How fantastic to suddenly
meet someone else with the same problems. She even gave me the right
word for the flavour of sweet things which I no longer liked —"metallic".
I'd always said "sour" but knew it didn't quite describe it right. So there
we were, both unable to recognise each other and both of us unable to be
the known person we both needed to be when out in social situations.*

*Initially we met up in very specific places using pieces of paper cut out
into the shape of a jigsaw piece each. I had the red piece and my friend
had the blue piece, matching the jigsaw pieces on the logo of the Encephalitis Society showing two pieces of life's jigsaw fitting back together. At
our meeting place we would both be checking for somebody holding their
paper piece, or having it next to them at a coffee shop somewhere—and
it worked! We have since bought a bag of loose beads and made ourselves matching necklaces which we now wear when we are meeting
together, and needing to stay together. A bit easier than our jigsaw pieces
and we look a lot less bizarre to the onlookers. Nicky and I did our training for the trek together and supported each other while preparing for it
(Figure 12.3). By the time we went on the trek we had moved on to using
our necklaces, much easier than a jigsaw piece up the mountain, and
we managed to trek together! We always wear them when we meet up
nowadays, giving us the security of our friendship together.*

Ed talked about Claire's ability to meet people, saying "She's far less
relaxed about meeting people she knows than people she doesn't know.
She hates much more going to meet people she knows she knows.
Whereas she's quite happy to talk to strangers on a train. In fact it's a

Figure 12.3 Claire (on the left), Nicky and Barbara taking part in Trek Transylvania with the Encephalitis Society.

remarkable feature of her that normally she'll go on a train journey and she'll tell us all about who she spoke to, complete strangers." Barbara mentioned to Ed a science evening in Cambridge that Barbara, Joe and Claire had all attended. Claire was the star and happily spoke to people. Ed responded, "But she will have a completely different viewpoint about that, I guarantee you. Her view will be that she was struggling and it was all terrible. And I know that's not just because she's negative because she isn't negative at all. It's because her assessment of the situation is completely different. And also, I've had this discussion, quite firm discussions with her about this and she totally disagrees with me, where I say, 'to the person you're speaking to, it doesn't matter that inside you're all ughhh. It doesn't matter at all, what they'll perceive is someone who's socialising perfectly well with them and for them, that's all that matters. You're being friendly and kind and everything that you are.' She completely disagrees with me. She says it does matter—what she's feeling. If we go out, say to a party, she'll have a good time dancing and so on but she will feel she's struggled and not had a good time. A lot of her perceptions are so warped now and that's why she doesn't see very much good. There's no beating it though." Barbara said to Ed, "Fergus tried very hard at the OZC. I get the feeling that at the time, it worked but now she's forgotten all that." Ed's answer was, "No, I don't think she has forgotten it. She hasn't forgotten the ways of dealing with it and she hasn't forgotten the things that people said to her. I hope we've tried to reinforce that but it doesn't make any difference to how she assesses it. You can alter what she thinks a little bit, if you go through situations and point out how well they went. But she doesn't count those. She discounts everything positive about what's happened and just considers the struggle, which is obviously great, but when she achieves whatever it was she was trying to achieve, the achievement doesn't count, just the struggle. So she has a negative viewpoint of what's happened."

Four years after the illness I was asked if I would help with some research work testing a new piece of equipment which was hoped would help people with memory problems. Over a period of months I wore the Sense-Cam and recorded events also written into a diary. The SenseCam is a small camera worn around the neck which takes photos with a fish-eye lens every 20 seconds or at any change in light or movement. The Sense-Cam loads the photos into a computer where they can be seen rather like an old home video, and although each photo is an individual shot, they do sequence very well. I reviewed these photos and my written notes at given intervals and the researchers did their testing about my memory capabilities.

Right from the beginning I was able to know that the event reviewed from the SenseCam later gave much better triggers to my memories than my written notes. The photos weren't the standard "tall at the back, short at the front, and SMILE!" photos, but very meaningful snaps of every moment, completely unstaged and they gave me a real sense of having been there, being part of it, and belonging. And the feeling of security of my memories has been the best bit. They're safe, in the computer and I can turn them on and re-live them whenever I like. The researchers' results showed that the SenseCam cues stimulated my episodic memory well, concluding that consolidating memories with the SenseCam led to more retrieval of new information, in particular sensory-perceptive details and cognitions, giving me a feeling of "being there" and "reliving". They felt that, although I was unable to consolidate new memories, the SenseCam imaging bridges this gap for me, allowing me to feel part of my own life. It felt great that the researchers were pleased with the positive results and an fMRI scan proved that this was right as my memory areas lit up with far greater activity when I was asked to think about events previously reviewed on the SenseCam.

I write notes into my SenseCam diary each time I use it and these words help me to understand vaguely what was happening and gives me some names to attempt to guess the individuals' identities. I have drawn table plans and seating arrangements with names, so that when viewing them I can have a chance of working out who might be who—as long as they don't change places of course. Nicky and I have been using ours together (Figure 12.4) and then watching each other's photos, having huge enjoyment in sharing our muddle of memories. As ever, we both have valuable memories to savour. I have safe memories with my Sense-Cam of travelling by train recently to stay with Nicky for the weekend. I

Figure 12.4 Claire (on the right) with her friend Nicky.

wore my SenseCam during the journey and had put my bead necklace on ready. I had the Encephalitis Society badge on my coat and had pinned my red jigsaw piece onto the other side of my collar, so that Nicky would have plenty to recognise me by. Identity is helped by body movements and facial expressions. Once, when I looked in a mirror with Nicky, I thought I was Nicky, until she told me that person was her.

On another occasion, I was looking back at my SenseCam pictures of me and my other friend Nikki (spelled differently), where I was being shown how to use the laptop to play a DVD. Nikki had asked me if she could wear the SenseCam for a change? That's weird!! She's looking a bit old, my brain is whirring! What ARE we doing? Hang on a minute, we're at her house now . . . and she must be wearing it again. It took me ages to realise it was me as I am not usually seen in the SenseCam pictures. I think it must be me, she's wearing blue and the person using the SenseCam has pink sleeves. And there is my son demolishing the twiglets. These are very powerful memories and the process of watching the pictures and reading my odd notes gives me a very real feeling of belonging to those events, those people, my own life. Cheers again.

Using SenseCam hasn't been easy every time. I have rather felt sometimes that everyone is looking at me, trying to assess who I am and what I am up to. I wonder if they might be thinking that I could be secretly assessing them. I have been served very quickly and politely in shops and cafes! I've coped with that worry and just decided that anybody can have items which attract the attention of others, so I mustn't feel self-conscious about wearing it. I must value it for myself and, if I am challenged or just asked about it, I can explain in simple words "It's a camera". If they want a better explanation I say "I use it to help with my memory problems." Full stop. No more eye contact. If they are someone I don't feel right sharing my story with, if they continue to be nosey, I try to change the subject and talk about the weather. Sometimes, I may decide that it is suitable to share information with this person. Last week Nicky and I were together and I needed a new lead to charge my Sense-Cam. Nicky needed one too. We found a man with a camera stand and I took out my SenseCam to ensure the lead I bought would have the right connection. He smiled and said to me "Memory?" I didn't launch straight into it but just said "It's great." I was thinking—it stores my memories for me, now that my brain can't manage that very well any more. I can now re-live them whenever I like—just like I used to before my illness, they're mine again. I use SenseCam nearly every day but not all day, having learned that washing up and the steering wheel are pretty boring things to watch back over and over again. I choose which events I want to be able to recall and I use it then. I make notes but these are just a memory jog into a world the SenseCam pictures take me right into.

I always choose to view the photos individually, rather than as a show, which is like a stilted home video. I find it amazing just how many memories and feelings get jogged from the slightest little thing in each photo and I find that access to my memories is much better when I look at each picture separately for as long as I wish. The photos in my albums don't tell anywhere near the same story as the SenseCam photos of daily life, with everyone laughing, teasing and elbowing each other, in the right order. Daily life storage. That's what SenseCam gives me—reality, safety!

Technology is evolving fast and I am one of the first brain injury patients to benefit from this fantastic new device. I'm also happy now that it is now marketed as a "Vicon Revue" for others to use and to give real security to their new memories. One of the researchers described my feelings about it, as a "Proustian moment"—that "a rope had been let down from heaven to draw me up from the abyss of unbeing." And after the research I was allowed to keep it!

Chapter 14

Paddling through the river and stepping on stones

An overall summary of my life since encephalitis

I am lonely. We all take for granted the concept of "self" without even thinking about it. "Myself" I do not know me anymore. Other people know themselves, and "me", and I know neither now. I feel like I have lost my heart as well as my head.

My life since the illness has been like seeing a film but starting half way through as if I were late. I don't know any of the individual characters or how they work together. I don't understand the plot or any of the actions happening or why. It is complicated and confusing but everyone else who saw the film from the beginning is able to understand what is happening and appreciate what may happen next. They understand the sarcasm and humour while I am there thinking that everyone is being nasty to each other. Because I don't appreciate how people are interacting together makes it hard for me to anticipate or understand what will happen next. Others have an understanding of the past which gives them thought and expectations about the future so they become able to have appropriate feelings about the plot and how the story unfolds. They are able to sense power and types of behaviour because of their background knowledge.

I need to stop trying to pretend to myself and others that I am the person I used to be. I need to work at being this "me" by using what understanding I still have and make the best of myself as I am now with no pretence.

Nowadays, 10 years on, my family love to tease me, deliberately watching with their smiles bursting to happen as they assess whether I have "got-it!" or not. I can tell more by their body language and eye contact that they're just waiting for me to misunderstand and react wrongly, but are happy to have a good laugh when the penny actually drops. And I don't feel threatened, I feel part of the gang now, which is nice.

I am making a visual memory of my life to remind me about myself and all parts of my life I have shared. I am using photos and written notes to complete the story and to put back together the jigsaw pieces of life in the best way I can. I want to understand my life as well as possible. SenseCam is helping me to store new and ongoing memories of how my life is progressing. It will help me hugely in the ongoing ability to build the jigsaw of my ongoing life with great strength.

The one thing I've learned from writing this book is just how much more I should be re-reading all my written notes of the advice I have been given and to try harder to live a much happier life by it. I know I can do this and I must be reminded to try! I am being realistic. Like it or lump it, this is how I am now. I accept what has happened and hope to continue going forwards and be a happy individual even though I am different from before. Sharing life with family and friends in a warm, caring, sharing way, I say "One life, live it" and put the past behind me. Crossing bridges is not always easy, but paddling through the river and stepping on stones can get us to the place we want to be.

I know it has been hard for my family and friends to accept and appreciate just how much my whole personality has changed. The person they knew just doesn't exist anymore. My family has to find me as I am now. Somebody very different from who I was. They have to live with my problems and when they have tried to help me by saying how I need to do things quicker or better, I have taken their support as nagging and criticism. This hasn't been fair on them but I feel frustrated and upset that none of them trust me anymore. Over time, Ed has supported me to manage the household itinerary and gradually taken things over himself to help all of us to settle down and cope better together. Dad has, therefore, taken control and our children always turn to him first. They don't expect me to manage well anymore, so they feel it is not worth them bothering me as I always get flustered and that is more bother than it is worth for them.

I have felt rejected, shut out of family life and of being a wife and a mum. It is not their fault and I am not blaming them as they have all tried to do their best to live alongside me. They have each become very independent. I know their independence is valuable for them but it has exacerbated my feelings of not being connected to them. I have lost the feeling of knowing them. I don't share my life with them and they choose not to share theirs with me, other than in a practical way like food, money, lists and clean clothes. Emotionally I feel shut out and separate from all of them. Any important issues or arrangements are shared with their Dad and I am not considered necessary or a part of them. To use my daughter's words: "You are just a bystander." That is me, left out and that is exactly how it feels now. I have very little sense of belonging to a life which I was very much part of but now have almost lost. I have no memories of my children being young and growing up. It upsets me hugely to hear other people *talking happily about fundamental, important parts of their lives or masses of minor issue memories just for fun. I no longer feel like their Mum.*

So I feel left out of family life. This isn't helped by my own difficulties managing noise and bright lights. I have been unable to watch television or listen to music with my family or join in with their leisure times. I haven't watched any TV since trying initially when I came out of hospital but it was impossible to follow any plot, not recognising any of the characters or remember what had happened only a few moments before, let alone understanding any of the humour in it. So right from the beginning I have kept out of our sitting room and based myself in the kitchen. I have enjoyed playing cards and have had many good times playing card games with my family and friends when I can persuade them! Games are much more straightforward and manageable for me than general chit-chat, which usually involves other people—and their life stories. I still play "patience" rather addictively, like Clive Wearing (see Chapter 1), but I still prefer to play games with my family and friends. And there's nothing like "Pass the Pigs", a quick "Bananagram" or even if I'm lucky, "PIT"!! Games to be played in the company of a group of people where the "rules" and "turns" are the subject of chat is much easier for me, and more manageable emotionally, than being asked the life story of "Pat". It's nicer to squabble about who won "Perudo" than who it was who wore the green hat ten years ago.

Our children have grown up throughout this period and some have left home already. This has been hard for me as I have been left out of supporting them to arrange things. At the same time I have felt relieved to keep out of all the responsibility of doing it. It is lovely to say that I have missed them and I have enjoyed them coming home and still wanting me to make "dippy eggs" for them. And doing it my way which I can do now without my list. OK, I'm a softie but it has been nice to feel my identity has been valued again. My respect for them has been strengthened so that we are all moving towards a more normal relationship again.

I still cling on to bits of my old identity. I iron just how my mum taught me. I make Marmite toast, kedgeree and dippy eggs just as I did before. I wear frumpy, dull comfortable clothing and sensible shoes, and I have a handbag full of anything and everything anyone might need.

The Centre runs a Users' Group (a group for ex clients of the Oliver Zangwill Centre) which I voluntarily choose to attend, feeling ready to offer my own time and support for their research programmes as well as the need for feedback and thoughts about changes that may be considered for the programme. It is also a chance for me to continue to attend and I feel secure just being there again in a place where I am understood, cared about and have a real sense of belonging. It is good to be able to offer support back to the unit. I am occasionally asked to share time with the current clients who have similar problems and value somebody else to talk to in a meaningful way.

Ed also said that the Users' Group was a very positive experience for Claire.

I have recently been to my uncle's funeral. I was taken by my mum and dad and one of my sisters, and her daughter came too. I had looked carefully and tried to make some meaningful record in my mind about recognising each of them. Their clothing was the main thing I tried to use to help myself but by the time we were surrounded by lots of close family and friends all happy and sadly greeting each other I had forgotten completely what items/colours/garments I was meant to look out for.

I hung close to my Mum. In a social setting like this it is normal for people to have very warm reactions when meeting up with each other and sharing support. In amongst this crowd of strangers were my cousins who had lost their dad, and their children who had lost their granddad. He's my mum's brother-in-law and a great friend to many people there. They greeted me happily: "Hello Claire! How are you? A man came over and began hugging me and before I had any chance of asking him his identity, he was asking me if I still played the LP he's given me for my 17th birthday? Well that felt quite awkward for me, not having any memories of him, let alone the LP. Eventually, our friendship was explained to me and I realised that he'd been a great boyfriend to me.

Everyone kept moving and changing who they were hugging and greeting, and I was close to tears. It feels so distressing to be so unable to greet and treat each person in a real way. I found myself trying to pass my own difficulties as much as possible by attempting to put the focus on them in the hopes of gaining some trigger so that I might guess their identity. So the answer to the happy "How are you?" can be "Fine, how are things going for you?" And then making eye contact in a questioning way, encouraging them to speak about themselves thereby allowing the instant crisis of my not recognising them a bit of a chance to cope better, with a moment to catch my breath and make all the decisions about what to say and in what way.

"Who the heck are you?" would probably make it quicker but just doesn't feel very sociable or caring. So, they are talking about themselves for a moment and before I know it, many other names are brought in and I need to hope that chance may be on my side such that something they say might trigger a memory, give me a vague chance of guessing their identity—but I do have to be lucky.

It feels fraudulent at this time when I'm seemingly happy, listening to them and almost behaving as if I know them. At some point I need to decide if they know that I won't know them, if they think I do know them, or if they presume I do but are giving me a chance in the hope that I'll get there without needing to be told—or if they are Fred Bloggs and couldn't give a shred if I know them.

I've lost Mum, my sisters, my dad and people are greeting me, and I've got no-one to ask. A little girl rushes up to me with arms out and we share a big hug and in that sudden decision-making situation it feels more urgent to ask, so I do: "Sorry—who are you?" She tells me her name and hugs me again. It's a name I've heard but it's not giving me the right connections so I ask her, "Who is your mummy?" She tells me and I get into even more of a muddle. By that time I'm thinking through lists of names which fit together in my memory, repeating over and over again family members, their partners and children, and it's almost a case of the syllables giving a ring almost poetically or musically, which I use to remind me of their identity and how they fit together. For example, "Jane, John, Jack and Georgina" fit together, the list has a ring to it and can trigger the memory of how they relate to each other, but then comes the worry as to how that unit of family is situated in the family tree.

I have drawn myself my own visual reminder of our family tree and use this to remind me as much as possible, but it isn't always sociable to have it out in front of me, even though in this instance it possibly could be. Groups of names have a ring tone in my memory bank and it's almost like singing a song to try and connect them together. But sadly, on this occasion this young lady had told me her name happily and that of her mum but neither rang together in a way I could connect them with my cousin because his name wasn't there and the ring tone of hers and her mum's didn't sound right without her dad and sister's names too.

Maybe in this instance I should be asking, "Who are your family?". But hoping she just wouldn't simply point them out to me. My consternation at not knowing her suddenly increased when she happily reminded me that I'd helped her with a psychology project she'd been doing and had given her some information about my SenseCam. That suddenly made it ten times worse, so I wasn't only wanting to connect her in the family tree but I'd had some personal, meaningful contact with her family recently, which I had no memory of whatsoever. However, there was no doubt she was happy about it, which was lovely.

It is a bizarre situation to be surrounded by people who know about my life over the years, months, days and minutes past, almost without me having had any past at all. They talk of it in a way I'm seemingly *supposed to know—which exacerbates the complications of not knowing them into a state of guilt for not having any memories which give under-standing of our lives together, our friendship and relationship.*

Old friends and new! Today I took my new friend's daughter to the drop off point, a short way from her school. She had arranged to meet her friend there but it was pouring down and she had art work so I offered to take them all the way. Her friend got into the back of my car with her paint-ing getting soaking wet in the rain. I was introduced nicely by my friend's daughter. Her friend said "I know Claire!". I didn't panic as it was said so happily and I felt reassured that one of them would enlighten me quickly as to who she was. It happened! My friend's daughter said the other girl was Marion's daughter. I remembered the name Marion as a special friend I've had for 20 years or more, but I didn't recognise her daughter or remember her name. I smiled happily at her and she must have known as she said to me "I'm Becky." That was lovely, and it made me very happy that she had said so. I felt secure of her family identity understanding and memories of her own character which were rather more instinctive than actual but I think her voice sounded familiar to me. I had to concentrate on driving then but was able to feel secure just knowing that Becky knew I didn't recognise her, and why I hadn't known her. She had been happy herself to remind me and cope with all my uncertainties. It felt lovely to have helped them both and they made me feel loved.

Enough of that! I am moving forward as a much happier person nowa-days with a lot more confidence, which has been given to me by all my therapists and all my family and friends. I think of myself as a very lucky person who has survived as best I could have thanks to my wonderful family, and all the wonderful people who have understood and supported me throughout. I'm using my SenseCam to record me tripping and falling but also succeeding to throw all the pieces of my life's jigsaw back into the middle with great relief. I am re-finding "myself". My body is fine, my brain is rehabilitated and my "being" is becoming clearer each day. Thank you especially to Barbara Wilson, as I see her as the integral cog in my rehabilitation and feel very privileged to have been in the right place at the right time for the postcode lottery of life.

Ed's comments on life now: "Obviously, Claire's illness has affected abso-lutely everything. And it's also affected all of *us*, all different parts of the family in different ways, although we haven't investigated each other in depth. Quite early on, actually at the Oliver Zangwill, so not that early on, but within a year or two, our oldest daughter said something really interest-ing which was—she said something because Claire was upset at not being a proper mum anymore because she couldn't do lots of things—and our daughter made a comment, that you're a better mum now as you're not at work the whole time and you're here at home. I suppose, Claire can only manage certain tasks, certain things in the house. Things you wouldn't initially think about. She can't manage to watch TV or films, something we used to do together. She used to watch things with the kids and enjoy stuff, so lots of things that normal families do are not available. On the other hand we sit around the kitchen table playing games more than we used to. So the dynamics of the family, I suppose those have changed significantly. It's certainly true that quite a few people in the family have taken on the positive sides of things. If you spoke to our older daughter now, she would say she grew up a lot, got a lot of experience and she wouldn't be the same person she is now if she hadn't had this experience. So there were positive things that happened in terms of the children's development. But it's hard for Claire, every single thing she does is anxiety-producing even though we know she does it fine. She goes to talk to schools and things and the sixth form are so receptive. She always does those things so well and gets fantastic feedback as well she should.

Figure 14.1 Claire and her pet duck (Peking).

Chapter 15

Final last thoughts

Life isn't easy for most people and many factors influence the pathways of our lives. When bad things happen, we realise just how much of a difference can be made by other people, whether they be family, friends, medical staff, police or an unknown person in the street. We can all make a huge difference to each other's safety, comfort and emotional well-being. I have tried throughout my life to care for everyone as I would choose to be cared for myself and feel that this is the way that real friendship is built. Memories may help but real value is in belonging. I want to share with you this lovely letter to me which I keep in my Friendship File, titled "For your memories collection". My friend begins by saying "This is Nina, with the brown curly hair and glasses." She then tells me how we met, about our children, and about the happy times that we have spent together. She goes on to talk about when she herself was unwell. She said "You took the strain out of everything for me and used to wake me up gently with a cup of tea. When I watched how you were recently with Helen when she was poorly and you were helping her, I thought, still the same very, very caring Claire." She finishes by adding "Well I hope this gives you a few memories. The main one to hold on to is that you are a fantastic friend. You are the most caring person, thoughtful and kind, with a wicked sense of humour. You are highly intelligent and loyal through and through." Like so many others, Nina has always been there for me.

I am much more prepared nowadays to manage my life with prosopagnosia but there is a continuous dread of meeting people who know me. I may react to them inappropriately and then they'll have feelings against me. It's a fear of losing friendship, which is a great worry for me. I'd hate anyone thinking that I was deliberately avoiding or ignoring them, as if I were choosing not to socialise with them. I think this need to care, and fear of being unsociable, is much stronger than people appreciate. Ed said to me recently that I always say that things are difficult for me but that no one ever notices or cares but they do! He's not there when the lady from 35 smiles and waves in my direction. Or when I'm at the swimming pool and someone says "Hello Claire! Are you coming for coffee?". I go and sit down with a group of smiling ladies who all know each other but don't know me. How is the nice lady feeling now that I've seemingly deliberately chosen not to have coffee with her today? People do notice my unexpected behaviour and they do care. I rely so much on the ones who do understand to go the extra mile to look after me and realise that I won't know them one moment to the next. These people give me the wide-eyed reassuring nod to comfort and reassure me—silently saying "I know you don't know me but it's OK, I'll remind you." It works the same way for me as somebody kindly noticing the difficulties and opening the door for somebody in a wheelchair, with a buggy, a walking stick, a suitcase or just too much shopping. It's an unspoken understanding, giving that bit of reassurance that makes all the difference.

These are my rules upon meeting me

- Smile. Tell me your name. Remind me of your identity.
- Uncover your name badge and throw me a line.
- Don't gather me up and move me along without explaining your reason. Remember, you're a stranger.
- NEVER say happily "Oh yes! I never remember names either!" (unless you have prosopagnosia, are attempting to show you understand, or have that part of your own brain deteriorating with age).
- Surnames help a bit but telling me where you live helps me hugely.

I know that I'm never going to be the same wife, mother, daughter, relative, friend or colleague as I used to be, because of my loss of memories. The thing that I do remember is that I have been extremely lucky and that there are very many people very much worse off than me. I may not be able to remember anything but at least I can see and hear when my family say they love me. I have a home, a happy family and friends all around me, with happy times to share. I have greatly valued my partnership with Ed and our shared parenting of our children, in our happy home together. Although we have had to change the structure of our life, the four corners of the jigsaw are now there. With the sides built strongly, I'm enjoying their help to "throw the pieces back into the middle!", as my son told me to do (see Figures 15.1 and 15.2).

Coming to terms with my limitations has been very stressful for me and "learning life the hard way" has become a normality. I have been

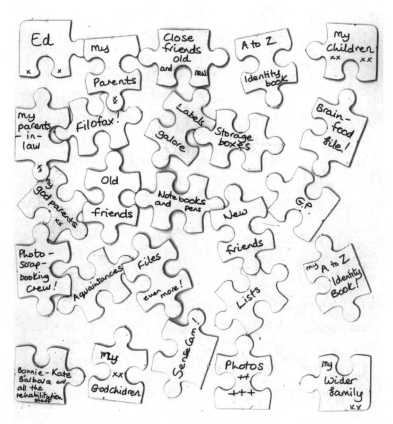

Figure 15.1 The jigsaw of my life before it fell apart.

supported by my rehabilitation programme to try and accept what has changed and use new ways to alter my behaviour accordingly, but I will only make the best of it when I properly learn to accept my limitations. The words on my final discharge notes say "inability to say no". I have survived the illness but not its consequences. I spend more time trying to "nurse" everyone around me. What I really need to do is to go back through my notes and advice sheets from all the therapists who have meant so much to me and remind myself of all the ways to "toe the line".

Homework: Make time.

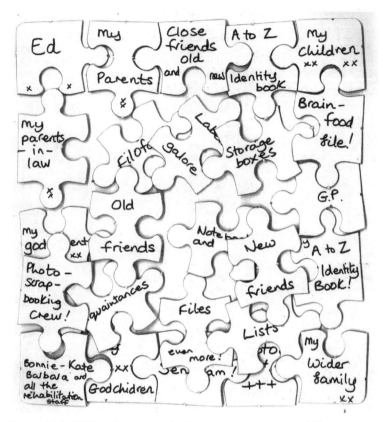

Figure 15.2 Following my wonderful rehabilitation our eldest son said to me "We've found the four corners now haven't we? And half the fun, well the whole fun really, will be throwing all the pieces back into the middle!"

Final comments: So what do we conclude about Claire's rehabilitation? Well she certainly did not recover but, as Claire says in her account, rehabilitation is not synonymous with recovery. Recovery means different things to different people. One interpretation is that recovery equals the complete reinstatement of the functions lost or impaired as a result of the brain damage (Finger, Levere, Almli, & Stein, 1988). For survivors of moderate or severe brain injury this is very rarely achievable. Another interpretation is the resumption of normal life even though there may be minor neurological or psychological deficits (Jennett & Bond, 1975).

This is certainly attainable for some survivors. Marshall (1985) defines recovery as the diminution of impairments in behavioural or physiological functions over time. This is likely to occur for the majority of patients. Kolb (1995), himself a survivor of a stroke, suggests that recovery typically involves partial recovery of function together with substitution of function. This is probably the definition of recovery that most closely reflects the situation for the majority of people who have survived an insult to the brain. It is also true of Claire; she certainly showed some early improvement (recovery) in the early days. Much of her success, however, was by substitution of function, that is to say she learned to compensate through the use of strategies.

Claire has a wonderful talent for self reflection. She is able to offer remarkably lucid descriptions of the nature of her challenges and how she adapts because of them. Not only are her accounts deeply moving, they also provide a rich source of data. The knowledge that she has lost, as well as the knowledge that she has retained, raise as many theoretical questions as they answer. Claire's is an expert account of the complex, and often ongoing, nature of rehabilitation that clinicians cannot afford to ignore.

To our minds, Claire is a remarkable person. Her prosopagnosia is extremely severe, her memory very patchy, and she struggles with many tasks yet she runs her house, she travels on public transport, she speaks publicly about her difficulties, she writes very well, she is extremely cooperative in any research or projects she is asked to participate in, and she is good fun to be with.

Barbara was on the trek to the Transylvanian Alps with Claire and 13 others in August 2010. We were raising money for the Encephalitis Society. It was a demanding and difficult trek with up to ten hours a day walking and climbing through challenging terrain. All of us completed the trek and Claire had little trouble keeping up. We collected several thousand pounds for the Encephalitis Society. She is a bright, socially skilled, caring person who has taught us much about living with face blindness.

As Claire is learning to believe, "We have one life. Live it."

Appendix I

A summary of Claire's one-day preliminary assessment at the Oliver Zangwill Centre

Claire and her husband came to the OZC for a one-day assessment in December 2004. We already had some background information on her illness and early recovery, together with reports from Bonnie-Kate Dewar, the neuropsychologist, and Claire's therapists. At the interview, Claire's husband stated that he was amazed how his wife had been persuaded to use lists and had become very organised. Claire showed us the diary she was currently using and in it were several slips of paper containing various lists for her meal planning. It was felt that this could be "fine tuned" with the help of our occupational therapists. Claire said, "I try and cook because I want to—I have to use a recipe—I can follow it."

She went on to say that she lacked motivation, she would sometimes look at her list and believe that she could not do it properly, which made her very emotional. This, in turn, left her feeling she needed to leave the tasks and rest, but resting made her feel guilty. She felt better if she rested but thought this was "wasting time". Claire indicated she was frightened of sleeping during the day because she already woke around 3 o'clock in the morning and she found this unpleasant because she felt unhappy when on her own. She experienced much anxiety, including symptoms of shaking, tearfulness, headache and pins and needles.

When asked what she hoped to gain from coming to the centre and what her goals might be, Claire said she would like to regain her self confidence, "return to being the friend I used be", recognise people, return to work and do it properly. She said, "I never wanted to be anything except a nurse" and she felt deeply about not being there to fulfil her role. She also wanted to drive and cope with a busy family life as her "role of mothering is difficult and partly taken away".

Claire's husband added that his wife needed to become better at understanding subtleties in communication. He said she struggled with things such as teasing, irony and sarcasm, which she often took literally. This makes understanding the interactions with and between the children more difficult for her. He went on to say that he would like her to become able to concentrate on more than one task. Finally he added, "If she wants to go back to work she needs to be able to reach the point where she is able to read complex articles. She finds reading difficult and watching television etc. almost unbearable, although I am not sure exactly why."

Claire had already had a neuropsychological assessment from Bonnie-Kate Dewar. A neuropsychological assessment helps build up a map of a person's cognitive strengths and weaknesses and identifies any emotional difficulties. The first assessment by Bonnie-Kate Dewar found that Claire had problems with memory, facial recognition, word recognition and retrieval, verbal abstraction, speed of cognition and visuo-spatial skills. Claire was reassessed in October 2004, to investigate her facial recognition difficulties in more detail. Further tests were carried out during the one-day assessment at the OZC to measure her speed of thinking, problem-solving skills, naming ability, other language skills and her perceptual capacity. We wanted to look again at her memory and attention abilities. Although very anxious, Claire was friendly and behaved appropriately throughout the testing; she seemed motivated to do her best. Once engaged in the testing her anxiety seemed to lessen a little.

Claire was almost certainly of above average ability prior to the encephalitis as she had good public examination results and was a state registered nurse. Several of her test scores were still above average, including her speed of thinking (speed of processing information) and her ability to carry out visual reasoning and visual problem-solving tasks.

With regard to memory functioning, Claire scored in the average range for immediate and delayed recall of prose (remembering a newspaper-type article). She also scored in the average range for immediate recall of visual material (remembering shapes and patterns) but was in the borderline (well below average) range for delayed recall of visual material.

The results suggested that Claire's memory for verbal information had improved since she was first assessed by Bonnie-Kate, probably due to some spontaneous recovery. Although, memory for verbal information was now one of Claire's relative strengths, it may still have been weaker than it was before her illness. Her immediate memory for visual information was also reasonably good, although she had problems with delayed recall and recognition of visual material. The pattern of results suggested that Claire had problems with the storage of visual information. This profile did not correspond with Claire's self-reports of memory difficulties, maybe because of the nature of the tests and possibly because the conditions in which testing took place are different from those she would experience in everyday life. It is also likely that Claire's loss of people knowledge made her think that her memory was worse than it really was and that her memory for verbal information was not so impaired as she believed. She, herself, said she forgot anything that was not written down. She was currently using a diary, lists, a filing system and photo albums to help with her memory.

Claire scored in the average range for sustained attention and at the bottom end of the average range for selective attention. This, added to her reported difficulties with attention (particularly dual tasking), suggested a possible decrease in her ability to concentrate.

There were no major problems with tests of planning and problem-solving. Claire was able to keep in mind the main goal of the task and complete tasks without breaking any rules. She demonstrated that she was able to plan, sequence and monitor her performance. She did not show major problems with executive tasks, suggesting her frontal lobes were functioning well. Her scores on many neuropsychological tests had improved since she was assessed by Bonnie-Kate in June, indicating some recovery.

Neuropsychological assessments identify cognitive strengths and weaknesses. Claire's main strengths were on tests of speed of verbal information processing, visual abstract reasoning, verbal memory, immediate visual memory and executive skills. Her weaknesses were seen on tests measuring delayed visual recall and the recognition of visual material. Claire reported and demonstrated a planful and strategic approach to problems, including both day-to-day practical memory demands as well as tests of novel problem-solving. These skills may be of particular use in her future management of cognitive difficulties.

Claire completed two mood questionnaires during the assessment period—the Beck Depression Inventory 2 (BDI) and the Beck Anxiety Inventory (BAI). On the BDI she scored 22/66, indicating moderate depression, and on the BAI she scored 39/66, indicating severe anxiety. These results seemed to correspond to her self-reports and her husband's observations. Claire described her mood as generally very low, often tearful, with low self-confidence. She experienced sleep problems including difficulty getting off to sleep and waking up early, together with loss of interest and feelings of hopelessness about the future. Her husband noticed that sometimes she can become overly happy. Claire's anxiety was triggered when she was alone. She said she had difficulty coping with her children and meeting people she didn't recognise. Tiredness made things worse. She felt cross and depressed with herself for not "being me and not coping with things properly".

Although she felt well supported she said, "I don't think anyone could stop me feeling this awful."

Speech and language assessment

Two naming tests were administered—the Boston Naming Test (Kaplan, Goodglass, & Weintraub, 1983) and the Spoken Picture Naming task from the Psycholinguistic Assessments of Language Processing in Aphasia (PALPA: Kay, Lesser, & Coltheart, 1996). On the Boston Naming Test Claire scored 50/60, and on the Spoken Picture Naming task from the PALPA she scored 38/40. These results are more than two standard deviations below the normal population showing that, despite some improvement, she still had some word-finding difficulties.

With regard to understanding spoken language Claire said she was easily distracted and could not concentrate very long on people's discussions. She did not watch television as she found it difficult to follow plots and change of characters. She said that background noise startled her and disrupted her ability to follow a conversation. She also had some problems with written language and was no longer able to read newspapers and books. Although she found some difficulty retrieving names of people, objects and places, she was able to communicate effectively. Her previous work involved good communication skills as she was involved in teaching and parental support. Her current social communication, however, was, she felt, impaired due to poor self-confidence, inability to recognise people, frequent bouts of tearfulness and an inability to recognise teasing and joking.

Claire's worries were due to identity change. She said, "Most of 'me' is really gone." This led to feelings of a loss of control, loss of choices and loss of opportunities in her life. She stated "I want to be me. I want to manage everything in my life as before. I want to work. I want to drive."

Assessment of physical function

Although there were no problems with physical mobility, Claire indicated that she experienced headaches and "body ache" when she was tired. Headaches were frequent and she was not sure if this was to do with her glasses. The headaches increased when she watched television. She also suffered from fatigue and said, "I have to make myself slow down and rest in the daytime, and I know I feel and cope better when I do." She had lost her sense of smell and had some difficulties with taste.

Assessment of activities of daily living and self-care skills

Claire was completely independent in self-care skills, she could plan and prepare most family meals, clear up and wash up, and could manage the laundry. With regard to child-care activities, she had no problems with parental care of her four children prior to the illness but now was no longer able to drive them around. She said, "Now I can't drive them around, otherwise I manage most things but not with as much confidence."

When asked about community activities, Claire said she did not go out alone due to lack of confidence. She said she could easily and quickly get lost and then get into a panic. She was very frightened of losing the person she came with and not being able to recognise them. She was able to go out to do the main household shopping for food if someone else accompanied her. She used a list to remember what she needed to buy. Financially, she did not receive any benefits and did not manage her own money.

When asked about her current activity level, Claire said she tried "to do too much and became tired quickly". She said she had a daily routine to get the children to school, complete household tasks, manage the cooking, resting and see friends.

The preliminary assessment report summarised the assessments and provided recommendations. It would appear that Claire's persisting difficulties are as follows.

Impairments:

- anxiety
- low confidence
- prosopagnosia
- noise sensitivity
- delayed visual memory
- possible attention difficulties.

Activity and participation restrictions:

- loss of vocational activity
- restricted participation in family life
- restricted community mobility.

To complete this preliminary assessment we organised an appointment with our neuropsychiatrist, in order to assess the need for medication.

This appointment was reported separately, and was sent directly to the GP. A prescription was provided on the day of the appointment, and Claire was advised of the likely time taken for medication to take effect (4–6 weeks), and possible side effects. Claire's husband said Claire was tried on a variety of medications which made her less anxious but also sleepy. She is currently on a better one, Sertraline. Bonnie-Kate Dewar, neuropsychologist at the Medical Research Council's Cognition and Brain Science Unit in Cambridge, was able to offer some input on alternate weeks in order to work on Claire's memory and face recognition deficits, but she felt that her input was not intensive enough to handle the anxiety difficulties that Claire was experiencing.

In light of Claire's assessment and current circumstances, we recommend that she return to the OZC for a Detailed Assessment in order to identify her rehabilitation needs and goals in more detail. Included in this would be specific assessments of the areas identified above, with a view to identifying specific long-term goals and whether these could be best met through an intensive neuropsychological rehabilitation programme or by some other means. We propose that this takes place around March time (when we will know if the medication has been helpful). As part of the assessment, it would be appropriate to organise a session in her own home, with an occupational therapist, to review her organising and planning system. It may eventually also be appropriate to organise a session with her family, perhaps to help address the feeling of guilt that Claire is experiencing. Further treatment options that may be of help include creating the occasional opportunity to meet with other clients known to us at the OZC with a similar spectrum of problems.

Regarding practicalities, Claire would be able to travel to Ely by train and a taxi would be able to collect her from the station and take her to the Centre. We discussed these recommendations with Claire and her husband and they are keen to pursue this course of action.

Later, Claire came for the two-week assessment and then funding was obtained from her health authority to pay for the full programme which she attended from November 2005 until July 2006. She attended the intensive rehabilitation programme four days a week for 12 weeks and then, after a one-week break, she came to the centre for two days a week for 12 weeks. This was the Integration Phase. She also attended work placements for two days each week. At the end of the programme Claire completed six half-days at the Centre (once a week) to discuss vocational placements, future planning, and how to apply the strategies she had learned at the centre. More details of the programme are provided in Appendix 2.

A summary of Claire's rehabilitation programme

The programme at the OZC is centred around goals. Clients, families and staff work together to determine meaningful and relevant goals to be worked on. The goals are negotiated so that, for example, if a client wants to recognise faces again and the staff feel this is not achievable, we will say something like "That may be a bit ambitious, what if we try to find a way to help you recognise some important people in your life?" As well as being meaningful and relevant, goals should be SMART, which is an acronym for "Specific, Measurable, Achievable, Realistic and Time based" (www.projectsmart.co.uk). See Wilson *et al.* (2009) for further discussion of goal-setting in rehabilitation.

Twelve goals were set for Claire in seven areas, namely (1) understanding brain injury (UBI), (2) cognitive rehabilitation, (3) psychological therapy, (4) communication, (5) independent living skills, (6) social and recreational skills and (7) occupational skills.

The goals for UBI were

1 Claire will rate herself as having a feeling of understanding of her brain injury.
2 She will have a full story of what happened, integrating medical information and a time line of other events whilst she was acutely ill.

The goals for cognitive rehabilitation were

3 Claire will specify nine people, and will be able to identify the faces of these people or will learn compensatory strategies by which to identify these people.
4 She will re-familiarise herself with memories of significant family events.

The goals for psychological therapy were

5 Claire will rate reduction in her rating of anxiety to be at an acceptable level.
6 She will rate an increase in her levels of confidence such that she is able to engage in identified activities.
7 She will alter her old, inflexible rules and develop new, more flexible and helpful rules consistent with a more positive sense of identity in herself and in identified situations.

The communication goal was

8 Claire will identify the communication consequences of her brain injury and develop strategies to cope with the impact of these on her everyday communication with her family, friends and colleagues.

The independent living skills goals were

9 The family will communicate together to understand their shared and individual needs and systems to support each other.
10 Claire will have an individual memory and planning system in place to allow her to plan and organise her week and complete 75% of planned activities.

The social and recreational activities goal was

11 Claire will have strategies in place to allow her to take photographs, label them, and attend her album group on a regular basis.

The vocational skills goal was

12 Claire will identify whether she can return to her job (or something similar) and have a written vocational action plan for 6–12 months following completion of the rehabilitation programme.

Significant progress was made on all the goals, even though not all were fully achieved.

With regard to her UBI goals, during the Intensive Phase of her programme Claire attended a range of educational groups, providing her with the opportunity to learn more about the consequences of brain injury and potential compensatory strategies. These group sessions were supported by individual sessions with team members, and, where appropriate, information thereby gained was applied to work towards the other practical long-term goals identified by Claire. She was also supported to develop her story of her injury. She also continued to attend a UBI group in the Integration Phase.

Claire decided to capitalise on her hobby of making scrapbooks and photo albums and make a "time line" of what had happened. She named it her "ABCD Timeline" as it was set out in chronological phases of her life:

- A—From childhood, nurse training, meeting Ed and having children, up to when she was taken to hospital
- B—Hospital scrap book, details of her brain injury and what happened while she was in hospital
- C—OZ album, her time at the Oliver Zangwill Centre
- D—Her personal journal, which she has been writing regularly with personal thoughts and possible ongoing adjustments after leaving the Oliver Zangwill Centre.

At the end of the programme Claire had not completed all of this timeline, but, with support, set up an action plan in her filofax to complete it at home and in her spare moments. This entails collating images, information from friends, the centre and family, and arranging this along a timeline. Claire is still working on this project.

Claire's ability to self-advocate had also improved. During the outcome meeting, at the end of the six-month programme, she was able to refer to her strengths and weaknesses following the injury in relation to possible work options. She had completed a written summary to support an occupational health appointment. Claire had been interviewed about her story for a radio series on memory, broadcast on BBC Radio 4, and also shared her story in the health section of a national newspaper. However, at times during the outcome meeting, for example when discussing her ability to manage a recent social event, she gave a negative account of herself that was not corroborated by her husband. This suggested that while Claire had developed a good understanding and awareness of the consequences of her injury, there were times when her experience or emotionally influenced recall of a situation resulted in her drawing negative conclusions.

One of the cognitive rehabilitation goals was fully achieved. This was identifying nine people or learning compensatory strategies to identify these people. Claire recognised that prosopagnosia or face blindness was one of her major problems. Bonnie-Kate had worked on face recognition problems for several months with some success at introducing compensatory strategies but no success in restoring Claire's ability to recognise faces. Consequently, given the challenge of accomplishing successful restoration of face recognition ability within the rehabilitation programme, it was decided to concentrate on the development of compensatory strategies to get round the problem. Over a period of five weeks, Claire worked with an assistant psychologist to develop mnemonics for person recognition. These mnemonics were in the form of short poems about the nine specified people, and linked personal information with visual information. The mnemonic for Claire's husband Ed, for example, was Ed "The Czech head—Oyster fed" (Ed's father was Czech and Ed loved oysters). Claire said she found working on these mnemonics enjoyable and interesting. She said it helped her to think about all the information she can use to identify people. Although she explained that she does not use the mnemonic strategy explicitly in daily life, she thought she was more aware of the specific characteristics of people. Furthermore, through this exercise she developed awareness of other characteristics that can be used to recognise people, such as their behaviour, the things they say, their hair, mouth and teeth, voice, and contextual information like the situation she might find them in. Subsequently, she both demonstrated and reported greater confidence in her skills to recognise people on the basis of non-facial information. On assessment, she was able to correctly identify 14 people as familiar or unfamiliar from their photographs when presented with 19 faces (four of which were distractors). She also reported some generalisation of this learning and recognised seven of nine people she had been unable to recognise in a baseline assessment. She looked carefully at cues such as face shape, eyes and hair of the people in the picture.

The mnemonics developed for the nine people Claire wanted to learn to recognise were typed up and given to her to refer to and learn. She liked having written information and wanted to have this to refer to. Claire was also given the structure used in the teaching sessions so she could apply it to new people and new situations. This included considering visual, verbal and contextual cues and then to link these to any semantic information Claire had about that person.

Claire appeared to find the process of the face recognition strategy as important as the intervention itself. In capturing the semantic information required for the mnemonics, she would often reminisce upon past experience with each face she was learning to recognise. She appeared to enjoy this and reported that things were "feeling special again", that she had "a good solid feeling about the past".

During discussions, a shared understanding of the person recognition process was developed. Claire said her ability to recognise people had been damaged: this is not solely the link between facial information and name, but is the process of facial recognition, access to personal information and subsequent person recognition, which provides a feeling of familiarity. She described a "storage box" containing personal information, from which she gained a feeling of familiarity when she was able to access it, but she was unable to access this through people's faces or their names. Sometimes she could access the semantic information through voice, or contextual information about the person. A compensatory strategy that Claire developed was the Friendship Book. She recognised that this book served to make the link between name and personal information, and gave examples of when she had used it. She said she would continue to use it for this purpose. (As we see later, Claire still uses the Friendship Book.)

In addition to the specific strategies described above, Claire said she felt sufficiently confident to explain her injury and ask people questions about who they are and that this enabled her to access personal information about them and gain a sense of familiarity when appropriate. She would, for example, ask "Where do I know you from?".

During the Integration Phase, cognitive work expanded to revisit executive skills and compensatory strategies discussed during the cognitive group in the Intensive Phase. Claire explained that she often felt overwhelmed, and found it difficult to apply strategies when this happened. She described a situation where she had a number of tasks to do during the day, but found it hard to prioritise and achieve any of her goals for the day. She recognised that this difficulty was, in part, anxiety-driven. She was advised to use the goal management framework (GMF; described in Chapter 12) to help her think about her "main goal" and to focus her activity on only one task at a time. These strategies are recommended as compensations for executive difficulties with planning, prioritising and dual tasking, especially when people are anxious. The interaction between executive difficulties and anxiety is likely to exacerbate difficulties with organisation, and the GMF offers a framework for thinking through one's goals.

Another of Claire's cognitive rehabilitation goals was for her to re-familiarise herself with memories of significant family events. However, her long period of retrograde amnesia, extending back to the time before her marriage, impacted on her feeling of belonging to her family. Overcoming this was a crucial aspect of her adjustment. Fortunately, there were family video tapes that could be used to re-familiarise her with memories that had been inaccessible previously.

Claire, herself, chose the specific family events and videos that she wished to re-familiarise herself with. She originally planned to watch videos with her family on a weekly basis, but was not able to consistently achieve this due to other family commitments. Despite this, she reported finding the experience enjoyable and rewarding and rated herself as more familiar with the events after watching the video. She said she used the family video collection as a strategy for preparing for a visitor she had not seen for a number of years, and described how this enabled her to access some other memories of the visitor.

Reassessment of Claire's autobiographical memory showed an improvement in her ability to recall personal semantic information compared to an earlier assessment 16 months previously. During the reassessment Claire felt her distant memories were more open to her and that she was able to remember "more normally" the earlier part of her life.

The psychological therapy goals were centred around anxiety and self-confidence. Claire presented with anxiety symptoms that were formulated in terms of the threat to her identity as a caring mother, wife, friend and nurse in a post-encephalitis world with its associated restrictions and changes. The formulation is described in the work by Dewar and Gracey (2007) and is reproduced with permission (Figure A2.1). Post-illness,

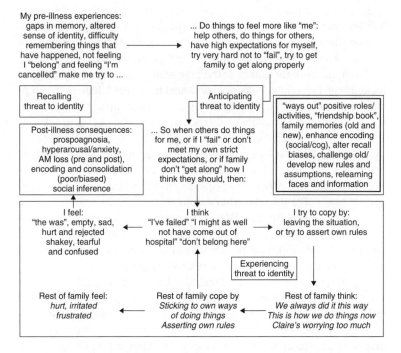

Figure A2.1 CBT formulation (with thanks to Fergus Gracey). From "Am not was": Cognitive-behavioural therapy for adjustment and identity change following Herpes simplex encephalitis (Dewar & Gracey, 2007, reprinted with permission of Taylor & Francis).

Claire felt unable to complete many of her typical duties, such as running the household or taking care of her children as she did before, and her anxiety symptoms further impacted on her low confidence regarding her functional abilities. Claire perceived a discrepancy between who she was before her illness and how she was defined post-illness. In the context of impairments in autobiographical memory, consolidation of new information and this perceived discrepancy, she attempted to do things to make herself feel more like "me" by the application of old, inflexible rules, and thus protect herself from this threat to her identity.

Based on this formulation, the mood goals for psychological therapy were developed. To address these issues, Claire had cognitive behaviour therapy (CBT) on a weekly basis. In addition, she attended the psychological support group and also received individual cognitive retraining sessions to address her face recognition and autobiographical memory problems.

Specifically, mood sessions sought to achieve the above-noted goals by building on work that had been undertaken prior to the OZC programme. A good therapeutic relationship had been established with Bonnie-Kate Dewar (supervised by Fergus Gracey), and Claire had been introduced to a CBT framework for understanding the relationship between thoughts, feelings and behaviour. Sessions continued to engage Claire in developing the formulation. At the beginning of her rehabilitation programme, significant anxiety symptoms presented a barrier to engaging in sessions and taking on information. She was provided with a brief relaxation exercise on a CD that was practised at the beginning of each session, to reduce her anxiety to allow her to engage in the session. Claire rated her anxiety before and after the use of the exercise, and generally rated her anxiety lower after the relaxation exercise.

Behavioural experiments (BEs) to test assumptions regarding particular situations had been attempted successfully prior to the rehabilitation programme and formed the principal vehicle for building confidence and reducing anxiety. An experiment was developed collaboratively by identifying an anxiety-provoking situation, identifying particular thoughts and/or assumptions associated with that scenario and then setting up a task to test the validity of that thought. This allowed the opportunity of developing new possibilities, new rules for living in these situations. The first of these BEs arose from a strategy for managing autobiographical memory deficits relating to friends, with the development of her Friendship Book, as described previously. Individual sessions continued to develop various experiments in addition to reflection of tasks in other sessions, such as monitoring non-verbal communication within the home or functional activities such as housework, shopping and cleaning. For example, Claire had expressed the rule that as a wife and mother she should be doing all the cleaning and shopping. However, she was able to break this rule by sharing the shopping with her husband, using a home delivery service and employing a cleaner. On reflection, breaking these rules did not mean that she had failed and she was able to observe that she felt more relaxed and confident working with her husband in these areas of their home life.

During the Integration Phase, rehabilitation tasks were developed within the team as "experiments for building confidence". A description of the task was provided as well as Claire's predicted outcome, and details of what actually happened. In individual sessions, she then reflected on what she had learned about herself from the task, in addition to compensatory strategies for managing confidence and cognitive difficulties. For example, an experiment was developed at her work placement at Wicken Fen (The National Trust nature reserve) regarding anxiety at being left alone with an unknown volunteer, with an outcome of strategies to develop conversations and feedback about her positive support. These exercises facilitated self-monitoring and awareness of others' feedback. Experiments also continued to be set within individual sessions, particularly relating to relationships within the family. For example, after an experiment on socialising at a party, Claire reflected that she was "able to have fun with her family" and that she has a lot of "experience being a Robertson". Attendance at a two-day nursing conference in Birmingham allowed exploration of her identity as a school nurse. Prior to the event, this was discussed within the framework of an "experiment for building confidence". Following the conference, Claire reflected that she was "still me", even though she had "lost a lot of knowledge", suggesting some incorporation of her pre-illness identity with her current self. Indeed, there was growing evidence of the normalisation of her difficulties, as she noted that other people at the conference also felt overwhelmed with information.

The CBT framework, incorporating behavioural experiments within sessions and across her rehabilitation programme, has allowed Claire to partially achieve her goals of reduced anxiety and increased confidence, as noted in her comments above. Indeed, by actively trying to do things differently and then reflecting on the personal meaning of the event outcome, Claire reflected that she felt more "at ease" with her friends, and that she was able "to cope", and to be "close" and "warm" with her children. She also described improved relations with her husband. She reported that although she still struggled to do things differently, she could see the benefit of thinking and acting in a more flexible way. Towards the end of the Integration Phase, she stated "I'm still me", with identification of strengths (socialising) and weaknesses (memory problems), which suggests development of a positive sense of identity in partial achievement of her third mood goal.

In addition to this qualitative report of positive outcome, Claire was reassessed on the Beck Anxiety Inventory (Beck, 1993) the Beck Depression Inventory (Beck, Steer, & Brown, 1996) and The Robson Self-Concept Rating scale (Robson, 1989). Symptoms of anxiety and depression remained at elevated levels, although these scores may at least in part reflect continued changes associated with the encephalitis rather than mood disorder. These were in contrast to Claire's subjective reports and self-concept ratings, which indicated an increase to a still reduced but significantly improved level of self-esteem.

At the end of the six-month programme, it was agreed that Claire would be seen as an outpatient to monitor her anxiety and support her use of a behavioural experiment framework for testing negative appraisals of situations and development of a positive sense of identity. The appointments would be at the OZC with Claire and her husband, aimed at supporting the extension of experiments into family and social life, with her and her husband collaborating on these. The aim of this was to facilitate less disagreement between them in their perspectives of her performance in key situations. Encouraging use of a specially prepared record sheet could be used to assist Claire and her husband with accurate monitoring of others' feedback, such as interactions within the family. The aim was to make Claire independent in the use of these strategies, with eventual cessation of sessions. Outpatient sessions would also reinforce the use of the mnemonic strategies for person identification, possibly incorporating this strategy into a confidence-building exercise.

Claire's communication goal was to identify the communication consequences of her brain injury and develop strategies to cope with the impact of these on her everyday communication with her family, friends and colleagues. Claire attended a weekly communication group in the Intensive Phase of the programme and continued with this in the Integration Phase. She also had weekly individual sessions. The focus of the communication group was on developing high-level communication skills, including presentation and debating skills. Initially, the group spent time analysing the debates they had carried out in pairs at the end of the Intensive Phase. This led to the establishment of specific individual short-term goals for each client. Claire considered her weaknesses were linking concepts in arguments, low self-confidence and poor planning.

The focus of the communication group was, therefore, on developing a planning strategy for delivering talks to facilitate linking in concepts during delivery, and to develop specific communication strategies for delivering the presentation. Claire initially wanted to deliver a lesson on healthy eating at the school where she had her voluntary work placement, but later realised that this would not be possible due to the level of difficulty of the children she would be seeing. She therefore agreed to demonstrate increased confidence through delivering a presentation to staff and clients at the centre about Wicken Fen, where she had a voluntary work placement. She successfully demonstrated planning skills and confidence in her presentation, receiving good feedback from her audience, thereby achieving this short-term goal.

Previously, Claire had identified low confidence as a factor impacting on her communication with her children; this was tackled in her individual communication sessions. Although, it was agreed that she would demonstrate her strategies to show confidence in the presentation task in the centre, she also experimented with these strategies at home and fed back the results in her individual sessions. The strategies discussed involved focusing on the non-verbal aspects of communication. These included eye contact, tone of voice, volume of voice, body language and gesture. At the start of the Integration Phase, Claire and her speech and language therapist, Leyla Prince, had watched a video of the progress meeting held with her family prior to the Integration Phase, and rated her non-verbal behaviours. She agreed that she had demonstrated low confidence, passive behaviour and the sense of being intimidated. She stated that this was unlike the person she was at the centre, and that she felt confident in the centre. We therefore agreed to experiment with changing some of these behaviours at home to see if it impacted on her relationship with her children. Claire experimented with making more eye contact with her children and speaking in a clear voice, raising her volume slightly. She reported that with making more eye contact, the quality of the interactions with her children had improved. She also quoted two examples of interactions where she felt apprehensive beforehand, but followed through anyway, and experienced a positive outcome. She thought the children were surprised by her approach, but recalled that her son had commented "You're much better than you were before." Claire said she felt very positive about this.

She also recognised how her own behaviour impacted on the interactions with her children. Towards the end of the Integration Phase, Claire and Leyla watched a second videotape of a family progress meeting and the difference in her behaviour was readily observed. There was still a slight uneasiness about Claire, but her non-verbal and verbal communication style had improved significantly. The importance of continuing to implement these changes in her communication style were emphasised to Claire in order to make the changes more permanent and automatic. She was therefore advised to continue to consciously apply these strategies in her communication with her family.

The first of the independent living skills goals was for the Robertson family to communicate together to understand their shared and individual needs and systems to support each other (this was covered in other goal areas), and the second was to have an individual memory and planning system in place to allow her to plan and organise her week and complete 75% of planned activities. Claire made significant progress in this goal area, made possible through combining the mood work to reduce her anxiety around her memory and face recognition problems with the independent living skills work. During the Integration Phase, work on Claire's memory system focused on helping her to plan her week in relation to the increasing demands on her time due to the voluntary work. Claire had a weekly session to review her plans for the forthcoming seven days and enable her to organise items in her "To do" list. Initially, at the start of the Integration Phase, it was observed that she was continuing to write items to do in her notes section and at times making the system more complicated by adding additional note pads. By consistent checking Claire was able to identify and reduce this complication. However, she maintained additional note pads for the different voluntary work placements. At times when these were discussed, Claire was able to acknowledge that the information she was recording was not in the most useful format, and she was able to independently consider how to improve this by having a more structured way of recording.

In addition, there were times when Claire impulsively wrote down information in random places when anxious. As a result of this, Claire was introduced to the "STOP THINK" strategy, whereby staff prompted her with these keywords when this behaviour was observed. This strategy was then expanded to PAUSE (stop), REFLECT (consider what you need to write down), SELECT (decide where is the best place to write this information that you will be able to find it again) and RECORD (write it down). Claire demonstrated independent use of this strategy in some circumstances. When her anxiety levels were high, however, she continued to require prompting to slow down and utilise the catch phrase.

In order to assess whether Claire was achieving 75% of her planned activities on a weekly basis, she was supported to transfer items "to do" into the calendar section of her filofax. Over a two-week period she marked off whether she achieved these tasks on the appropriate date in her diary. The results indicated that Claire was successfully achieving her targets at least 75% of the time, so this goal was considered to be achieved. Time was spent with Claire writing out the details of her memory system. Claire talks about her memory system, including what she uses now, in Chapter 11.

We thought that Claire's memory system might need to adapt and change as her roles and needs changed. During her time at the centre we noticed that she began to add more entries into the diary section of her filofax and was, therefore, considering changing the sheets from a week over two pages to one day per page. It was decided to check on this at the review meeting planned for Claire following her discharge from the centre and to tell Bonnie-Kate Dewar, who was monitoring Claire on a regular basis.

The strategy of "pause, reflect, select, record" was extended to a more general strategy of "pause, reflect, relax, connect" (PRRC). This was a cue for Claire to step back and reflect on the strategies that she had developed and practised to cope with situations, one of these strategies being relaxation. Here "connect" referred to connecting to and implementing the strategies. It was recommended that in busy, or novel, situations, Claire should continue to use PRRC to enable her to maximise her executive skills.

The social and recreational activities goal was for Claire to have strategies in place to allow her to take photographs, label them, and attend her album group on a regular basis. This goal overlapped with the UBI goal when Claire decided to do an ABCD "time line". Under the social and recreational activities she progressed with minimal guidance and support. In the Integration Phase she took photos and was able to label them according to the location, the event and who was in the photograph by referring to a notebook system in which she recorded the details each time she took a photograph. She independently located a postal service to send her photographs off to get developed, as she was currently unable to drive. Once the photographs were returned to her she created a new scrapbook containing the photographs. This scrapbook detailed some of the events that occurred during her six-month programme, including trips out with other clients and her voluntary work placements. Claire also said she wanted to attend her album group twice during the Integration Phase. Once the Integration Phase was completed, the Red Group kept in touch with each other for many months.

Claire also wanted to organise her old photographs into boxes/envelopes according to the year they were taken. Because of her prosopagnosia she acknowledged that she required support from friends or family members to label the photographs correctly. Claire started work on this and sorted them into years. During the Integration Phase, however, she was not able to find the time to sit down with someone to label them in relation to the people in the photos and what the events were. She began work in relation to her UBI goal, creating a time line of photographs of events in her early life, but this has yet to be completed. She has a large number of photographs, so this is an ongoing goal, which Claire still appears motivated to complete.

The final goal was to do with vocation. Claire really wanted to be able to call herself a nurse and often said she was born to be a nurse. The goal was that Claire should identify whether she can return to her job (or something similar) and have a written vocational action plan for 6–12 months following completion of the rehabilitation programme.

During the Integration Phase Claire went on two voluntary work placements each week. The first was to the Education Department at the National Trust's Wicken Fen site. Her duties varied from clearing sheds, mending nets, preparing teaching materials, to working with the children on activities, primarily pond dipping. Initially, Claire was accompanied by our rehabilitation assistant. However, six weeks into the placement she went on her own. Feedback—using a Work Behaviours Evaluation Form, which looks at attendance, productivity, work attitude, interpersonal work behaviours (supervisors), interpersonal work behaviours (colleagues)—from her supervisors was very positive. Claire was rated from good to excellent for the majority of categories. While on placement she worked well with staff, volunteers and children. Towards the end of the placement she was seen to be independently managing her fatigue (i.e. she would say when she needed to take a break).

The second weekly volunteer placement was at a school for children with learning difficulties. Claire was familiar with this school as she had been there as a senior school nurse prior to her illness. She worked within the Blue Room, which looked after the most challenging pupils in the school. Her duties involved working one to one with pupils either in the classroom or in the community, ensuring their needs were met. The feedback was also very positive, being rated excellent in all categories.

The voluntary work placements were considered to be a valuable part of Claire's rehabilitation. They gave her the opportunity to identify, implement and evaluate strategies within supportive environments. The feedback confirmed her own thoughts of her strengths, which were to always give her best, be enthusiastic and happy, have excellent communication skills with a variety of people including children, know her abilities, and be able to ask for advice and assistance when needed. The whole experience increased Claire's confidence and self-worth in relation to work settings.

Towards the end of the Integration Phase Claire attended a two-day Royal College of Nursing conference in Birmingham. Her reasons for going were to ascertain what nursing knowledge she had retained and to be among nurses again. Claire was able to evaluate what she had gained from the experience. She felt the positives related to her being able to travel independently and to find her way around, feeling sufficiently confident to speak to other delegates as an equal, socialising with delegates in the evening, able to attend all sessions, and being comfortable with the fact that she was on her own. On the negative side she described the lectures as being too complex, she took notes as well as website addresses but had not followed these up. She found it upsetting that she did not have the knowledge that she felt she should have. In some instances, words or phrases were familiar to her but they held no meaning. Claire had implemented strategies for managing her fatigue that she had learned at the centre but found she was very tired at the end of the day.

Claire had an appointment with an occupational health consultant in July and worked with Sue Brentnall, her occupational therapist, to prepare for this. Claire was able to prepare notes that summarised her progress since her last appointment five months before. She noted that return to her previous role was unrealistic and the way ahead, endorsed by the centre, was to continue increasing her confidence through gradually increasing demands in supported situations, such as voluntary work.

The following week, Claire, her husband, an employer, a representative from Human Resources, a representative from the Royal College of Nursing and Sue Brentnall, occupational therapist from the OZC, met. Claire was able to explain her progress to date without referring to any written notes. The representative from Human Resources said that from the information they had received from the occupational health consultant, the only option available to them as an employer was to retire Claire on ill-health grounds. There were no opportunities within their Health Care Trust to re-deploy her. Claire was reassured that her employers would support her through this process. Due to the nature of the retirement, the Human Resources representative felt it appropriate to put the vocation work at the centre on hold until it had all gone though. Claire and Sue discussed this after the meeting had ended. It was agreed that once the process had been completed Claire and Sue would see how Claire wanted to proceed in relation to work. In the meantime, Claire felt she could use the time as an opportunity to complete the work she had been doing at the centre on her timeline, go through her photos, offer to listen to readers at her local school, clear out her loft, and enrol on a creative writing course.

At the end of the six-month programme the staff felt that Claire had made excellent progress towards achieving her long-term goals. She was much better at managing her anxiety, she was more flexible, and had learned to deal with unhelpful ways of coping. She had improved and refined her memory and planning systems. She had developed an increased understanding of the encephalitis and its consequences, and this understanding has been shared with her family, who developed a broader understanding of the impact the illness has had on them all. Plans regarding future work options were still being discussed with a future meeting planned with her employer.

Claire appeared to be more relaxed and confident, and her husband agreed with this. However, she still held a negative perception of herself at times and it was felt that this area needed further work in order to facilitate a more positive sense of herself.

There was no doubt that Claire had made considerable gains and that she needed support to make further progress.

The following recommendations were made at the end of the six-month programme:

1   Claire and her husband to attend the centre to review their work together on sharing a more accurate account of Claire's roles and abilities at home and socially, in order to help support her work on emotional adjustment.
2   Claire to continue to see Bonnie-Kate Dewar for help with face recognition problems and coping with emotional difficulties.
3   Claire to meet with employer in July at her home to discuss retirement on ill-health grounds, as it was not possible for her to be redeployed in the Health Care Trust she had been working for at the time of her illness.
4   Vocational work that had been planned to be carried out at the centre should be put on hold until she had met with her employer and the situation clarified.
5   On completion of this decision-making process, Claire should return to the centre to meet with Susan Brentnall, occupational therapist, to discuss the vocational options.

Following her discharge from the OZC, Claire was referred to Dr Lizzie Doherr, chartered clinical neuropsychologist in the Peterborough Brain Injury Team, for further support.

References

Adler, A. (1944). Disintegration and restoration of optic recognition in visual agnosia. *Archives of Neurology and Psychiatry*, 51, 243–259.

Adler, A. (1950). Course and outcome of visual agnosia. *Journal of Nervous and Mental Disease*, 111, 41–51.

Allport, D. A. (1985). Distributed memory, modular systems and dysphasia. In S. K. Newman (Ed.), *Current perspectives in dysphasia* (pp. 32–60). Edinburgh: Churchill Livingstone.

Baddeley, A. D. & Wilson, B. A. (1986). Amnesia, autobiographical memory and confabulation. In D. Rubin (Ed.), *Autobiographical memory* (pp. 225–252). Cambridge: Cambridge University Press.

Balaban, M. T. & Waxman, S. R. (1997). Do words facilitate object categorization in 9-month-old infants. *Journal of Experimental Child Psychology*, 64, 3–26.

Barbarotto, R., Capitani, E., Spinnler, H., & Trivelli, C. (1995). Slowly progressive semantic impairment with category specificity. *Neurocase*, 1, 107–119.

Barry, S. R. (2011). Foreword. In P. S. Suter & L. S. Harvey (Eds.), *Vision rehabilitation: Multidisciplinary care of the patient following brain injury* (pp. vii–ix). Boca Raton, FL: CRC Press.

Barton, J. J. S., Press, D. Z., Keenan, J. P., & O'Connor, M. (2002). Lesions of the fusiform face area impair perception of facial configuration in prosopagnosia. *Neurology*, 58, 71–78.

Bate, S., Bennetts, R., Mole, J., Ainge, J., Gregory, N., Bobak, A., & Bussunt, A. (under consideration). Rehabilitation of face-processing skills in an adolescent with prosopagnosia: Evaluation of an online perceptual training programme *Neuropsychological Rehabilitation*.

Beck, A. T. (1993). *Beck anxiety inventory*. San Antonio, TX: Harcourt Assessment, Inc.

Beck, A. T., Steer, R. A., & Brown, G. K. (1996). *Beck Depression Inventory—11 Inventory*. San Antonio, TX: Harcourt Assessment, Inc.

Behrmann, M., & Avidan, G. (2005). Congenital prosopagnosia: Face-blind from birth. *Trends in Cognitive Sciences*, 9, 180–187.

Behrmann, M., Avidan, G., Marotta, J., & Kimchi, R. (2005). Detailed exploration of face-related processing in congenital prosopagnosia: 2. Functional neuroimaging findings. *Journal of Cognitive Neuroscience*, 17, 1150–1167.

Behrman, M., Peterson, M. A., Moscovitch, M., & Suzuki, S. (2006). Independent representation of parts and the relation between them: Evidence from integrative agnosia. *Journal of Experimental Psychology: Human Perception & Performance*, 32, 1169–1184.

Benjamin, C., Anderson, V., Pinczower, R., Leventer, R., Richardson, M., & Nash, M. (2007). Pre- and post-encephalitic neuropsychological profile of a 7 year old girl. In B.-K. Dewar & W.H. Williams (Eds.). *Encephalitis: Assessment and rehabilitation across the lifespan: Neuropsychological Rehabilitation Special Issue*, 17, 528–550.

Bennett-Levy, J., Butler, G., Fennell, M., Hackman, A., Mueller, M., & Westbrook, D. (Eds.). (2004). *Oxford guide to behavioural experiments in cognitive therapy*. Oxford: Oxford University Press.

Benton, A. L. & Van Allen, M. W. (1968). Impairment in facial recognition in patients with cerebral disease. *Cortex*, 4, 344–358.

Ben-Yishay, Y. (2008). Foreword. In F. Gracey & T. Ownsworth (Eds.), *The self and identity in rehabilitation: Neuropsychological Rehabilitation*, 18, 513–522.

Berry, E., Kapur, N., Williams, L., Hodges, S., Watson, P., Smyth, G., Srinivasan, J., Smith, R., Wilson, B. A., & Wood, K. (2007). The use of a wearable camera, SenseCam, as a pictorial diary to improve autobiographical memory in a patient with limbic encephalitis: a preliminary report. In Dewar B.-K. & Williams W.H. (Eds.), *Encephalitis: Assessment and Rehabilitation Across the Lifespan: Neuropsychological Rehabilitation Special Issue*, 17, 582–601.

Blonder, L. X., Bowers, D., & Heilman, K. M. (1991). The role of the right hemisphere in emotional communication. *Brain*, 114, 1115–1127.

Bodamer, J. (1947). Die Prosopagnosie. *Archiv für Psychiatrie und Nervenkrankheiten*, 179, 6–53.

Bornstein, B. (1963). Prosopagnosia. In L. Halpem (Ed.). *Problems of dynamic neurology* (pp. 283–318). Jerusalem: Hadassah University.

Brinthaupt, T. M. & Lipka, R. P. (1992). *The self: Definitional and methodological issues*. Albany, NY: State University of New York.

Bruce, V. & Young, A. W. (1986). Understanding face recognition. *British Journal of Psychology*, 77, 305–327.

Bruce, V. & Young, A. W. (1998). *In the eye of the beholder: The science of perception*. Oxford: Oxford University Press.

Brunsdon, R., Coltheart, M., Nickels, L., & Joy, P. (2006). Developmental prosopagnosia: A case analysis and treatment study. *Cognitive Neuropsychology*, 23, 822–840.

Bruyer, R., Laterre, C., Seron, X., Feyereisen, P., Strypstein, E., Pierrard, E., & Rectem, D. (1983). A case of prosopagnosia with some preserved covert remembrance of familiar faces. *Brain and Cognition*, 2, 257–284.

Burton, A. M. (1998). A model of human face recognition. In J. Grainger & A. M. Jacobs (Eds.), *Localist connectionist approaches to human cognition* (pp. 75–100). Hillsdale, NJ: Erlbaum.

Burton, A. M., & Bruce, V. (1990). Understanding face recognition with an interactive activation model. *British Journal of Psychology*, 81, 361–380.

Burton, A. M., & Bruce, V. (1993). Naming faces and naming names: Exploring an interactive activation model of person recognition. *Memory*, 1, 457–480.

Burton, A. M., Bruce, V., & Hancock, V. (1999). From pixels to people: A model of familiar face recognition. *Cognitive Science*, 23, 1–31.

Cahalan, S. (2012). *Brain on fire: My month of madness*. London: Allen Lane.

Calder, A. J. & Young, A. W. (2005). Understanding the recognition of facial identity and facial expression. *Nature Reviews Neuroscience*, 6, 641–651.

Calder, A. J., Lawrence, D. A., & Young, A. W. (2001). Neuropsychology of fear and loathing. *Nature Reviews Neuroscience*, 2, 352–363.

Cantor, J. B., Ashman, T. A., Schwartz, M. E., Gordon, W. A., Hibbard, M. R., Brown, M., . . . Cheng, Z. (2005). The role of self-discrepancy theory in understanding post-traumatic brain injury affective disorders: A pilot study. *Journal of Head Trauma Rehabilitation*, 20, 527–543.

Caramazza, A. & Shelton, J. R. (1998). Domain-specific knowledge systems in the brain: The animate–inanimate distinction. *Cognitive Neuroscience*, 10, 1–34.

Caramazza, A., Hillis, A., Rapp, B. C., & Romani, C. (1990). The multiple semantic hypothesis: Multiple confusions. *Cognitive Neuropsychology*, 7, 161–189.

Carney, R. & Temple, M. (1993). Prosopanomia? A possible category-specific anomia for faces. *Cognitive Neuropsychology*, 10, 185–195.

Carroll, L. (1871). *Through the looking glass and what Alice found there*. London: Macmillan.

Cooper-Evans, S., Alderman, N., Knight, C., & Oddy, M. (2008). Self-esteem as a predictor of psychological distress after severe acquired brain injury: An exploratory study. *Neuropsychological Rehabilitation*, 18, 607–626.

Coslett, H. B. & Saffran, E. M. (1989). Preserved object recognition and reading comprehension in optic aphasia. *Brain*, 112, 1091–1110.

Coslett, H. B. & Saffran, E. M. (1992). Optic aphasia and the right hemisphere: A replication and extension. *Brain and Language*, 43, 148–161.

Crawford, J. R. & Garthwaite, P. H. (2002). Investigation of the single case in neuropsychology: Confidence limits on the abnormality of test scores and test score differences. *Neuropsychologia*, 40, 1196–1208.

Damasio, A. R. (1989). Time-locked multiregional retroactivation: A systems level proposal for the neural substrates of recall and recognition. *Cognition*, 33, 25–62.

Damasio, A. R. (1990). Category-related recognition defects as a clue to the neural substrates of knowledge. *Trends in Neuroscience*, 13, 95–98.

Damasio, A., Damasio, H., & Van Hoesen, G. W. (1982). Prosopagnosia: Anatomic basis and behavioral mechanisms. *Neurology*, 32, 331–341.

Damasio, A. R., Damasio, H., Tranel, D., & Brandt, J. P. (1991). Neural regionalization of knowledge access: Preliminary evidence. In *Proceedings of the Cold Spring Harbor Symposia on Quantitative Biology*, vol. 55 (pp. 1039–1047). Woodbury, NY: Cold Spring Harbor Laboratory Press.

Damasio, H., Grabowski, T. J., Tranel, D., Hichwa, R. D., & Damasio, A. R. (1996). A neural basis for lexical retrieval. *Nature*, 380, 499–505.

Damasio, H., Tranel, D., Grabowski, T. J., Adolphs, R., & Damasio, A. R. (2004). Neural systems behind word and concept retrieval. *Cognition*, 92, 179–229.

Davidoff, J. & Wilson, B. A. (1985). A case of associative visual agnosia showing a disorder of pre-semantic visual classification. *Cortex*, 21, 121–134.

Davison, K. L., Crowcroft, N. S., Ramsay, M. E., Brown, D. W., & Andrews, N. J. (2003). Viral encephalitis in England, 1989–1998: What did we miss? *Emerging Infectious Diseases*, 9, 234–240.

DeGutis, J. M., Bentin, S., Robertson, L. C., & D'Esposito, M. (2007). Functional plasticity in ventral temporal cortex following configural training with faces in a congenital prosopagnosic. *Journal of Cognitive Neuroscience*, 19, 1790–1820.

De Haan, E. H. F. (1999). *Covert recognition and anosognosia in prosopagnosic patients*. Hove: Psychology Press.

De Haan, E. H. F., Young, A. W., & Newcombe, F. (1987). Face recognition without awareness. *Cognitive Neuropsychology*, 4, 385–415.

De Haan, E. H. F., Young, A. W., & Newcombe, F. (1991). Covert and overt recognition in prosopagnosia. *Brain*, 114, 2575–2591.

De Renzi, E. (1986a). Prosopagnosia in two patients with CT scan evidence of damage confined to the right hemisphere. *Neuropsychologia*, 24, 385–389.

De Renzi, E. (1986b). Current issues in prosopagnosia. In H. D. Ellis, M. A. Jeeves, F. Newcombe, & A. W. Young (Eds.), *Aspects of face processing* (pp. 243–252). Dordrecht: Martinus Nisoff.

De Renzi, E., Faglioni, P., Grossi, D., & Nichelli, P. (1991). Apperceptive and associative forms of prosopagnosia. *Cortex*, 27, 231–221.

Derogatis, L. R. (1983). *SCL-90-R*. Towson, MD: Clinical Psychometric Research.

Dewar, B.-K. & Gracey, F. (2007). "Am not was": Cognitive-behavioural therapy for adjustment and identity change following *Herpes simplex* encephalitis. In B.-K. Dewar & W. H. Williams (Eds.), *Encephalitis: Assessment and rehabilitation across the lifespan: Neuropsychological Rehabilitation Special Issue*, 17, 602–620.

Dewar, B.-K., Patterson, K., Wilson, B. A., & Graham, K. S. (2009). Reacquisition of person knowledge in semantic memory disorders. *Neuropsychological Rehabilitation*, 19, 383–421.

Douglas, J. M. (2013). Conceptualizing self and maintaining social connection following severe traumatic brain injury. *Brain Injury*, 27, 60–74.

Dowell, E., Easton, A., & Solomon, T. (2000). *Consequences of encephalitis*. Malton: The Encephalitis Society.

Duchaine, B. (2003). Dissociations of visual recognition in a developmental agnosic: Evidence for separate developmental processes. *Neurocase*, 9, 380–389.

Duchaine, B. (2008). Comment on prevalence of hereditary prosopagnosia (HPA) in Hong Kong Chinese population. *American Journal of Medical Genetics*, A, 2860–2862.

Duchaine, B., Yovel, G., Butterworth, E. J., & Nakayama, K. (2006). Prosopagnosia as an impairment to face-specific mechanisms: Elimination of the alternative hypotheses in a developmental case. *Cognitive Neuropsychology*, 23, 714–747.

Duchaine, B., Germine, L., & Nakayama, K. (2007). Family resemblance: Ten family members with prosopagnosia and within-class object agnosia. *Cognitive Neuropsychology*, 24, 419–430.

Dumont, C. (2013). Identity. In J. H. Stone & M. Blouin (Eds.), *International encyclopedia of rehabilitation*. Available online at http://cirrie.buffalo.edu/encyclopedia/en/article/156/

Duncan, J. (1986). Disorganisation of behaviour after frontal lobe damage. *Cognitive Neuropsychology*, 3, 271–290.

Ekman, P. & Friesen, W. V. (1976). *Pictures of facial affect*. Palo Alto, CA: California Consulting/Psychology Press.

Ellis, H. & Young, A. W. (1988). Training in face-processing skills for a child with acquired prosopagnosia. *Developmental Neuropsychology*, 4, 283–294.

Ellis, H., Young, A. W. & Critchley, E. (1989). Loss of memory for people following temporal lobe damage. *Brain*, 112, 1469–1483.

Emslie, H., Wilson, B. A., Quirk, K., Evans, J., & Watson, P. (2007). Using a paging system in the rehabilitation of encephalitic patients. *Neuropsychological Rehabilitation*, 17, 567–581.

Evans, J. J., Heggs, A. J., Antoun, N., & Hodges, J. R. (1995). Progressive prosopagnosia associated with selective right temporal lobe atrophy. A new syndrome? *Brain*, 118, 1–13.

Farah, M. (1990). *Visual agnosia: Disorders of object recognition and what they tell us about normal vision*. Cambridge, MA: MIT Press.

Farah, M. (2004). *Visual agnosia*, 2nd edn. Cambridge, MA: MIT Press.

Feinberg, T. E. (2011). Neuropathologies of the self: Clinical and anatomical features. *Consciousness and Cognition*, 20, 75–81.

ffytche, D., Blom, J. D., & Catani, M. (2010). Disorders of visual perception. *Journal of Neurology, Neurosurgery & Psychiatry*, 81, 1280–1287.

Fine, D. R. (2011). We need a simple test for prosopagnosia. [Review]. *British Medical Journal*, 342, 710.

Finger, S., Levere, T. E., Almli, C. R., & Stein, D. G. (1988). *Brain injury and recovery: Theoretical and controversial issues*. New York, NY: Plenum Press.

Fodor, J. (1975). *The language of thought*. Cambridge, MA: Harvard University Press.

Fodor, J. (1987). *Psychosemantics: The problem of meaning in the philosophy of mind*. Cambridge, MA: MIT Press.

Francis, D. R., Riddoch, M. J., & Humphreys, G. W. (2002). Who's that girl? Prosopagnosia, person based semantic disorder, and the reacquisition of face identification. *Neuropsychological Rehabilitation*, 12, 1–26.

Freeman, M. (1992). Self as narrative: The place of life history in studying the life history in studying the life span. In T. M. Brinthaupt & R. P. Lipka (Eds.), *The self: Definitional and methodological issues* (pp. 15–43). Albany, NY: State University of New York Press.

Fujii, T., Yamadori, A., Endo, K., Suzuki, K., & Fukatsu, R. (1999). Disproportionate retrograde amnesia in a patient with *Herpes simplex* encephalitis. *Cortex*, 35, 599–614.

Gainotti, G. (2004). A metanalysis of impaired and spared naming for different categories of knowledge in patients with a visuo-verbal disconnection. *Neuropsychologia*, 42, 299–319.

Gainotti, G. (2006). Anatomical, functional and cognitive determinants of semantic memory disorders. *Neuroscience and Biobehavioural Reviews*, 30, 577–594.

Gainotti, G. (2007). Different patterns of famous people recognition disorders in patients with right and left anterior temporal lesions: A systematic review. *Neuropsychologia*, 45, 1591–1607.

Gainotti, G. (2013). Is the right anterior temporal variant of prosopagnosia a form of 'associative prosopagnosia' or a form of 'multimodal person recognition disorder'? *Neuropsychology Review*, 23, 99–110.

Gainotti, G., Barbier, A., & Marra, C. (2003). Slowly progressive defect in recognition of familiar people in a patient with right anterior temporal atrophy. *Brain*, 126, 792–803.

Gainotti, G., Ferraccioli, M., Quaranta, D., & Marra, C. (2008). Cross-modal recognition disorders for persons and other unique entities in a patient with right fronto-temporal degeneration. *Cortex*, 44, 238–248.

Gallese, V. & Lakoff, G. (2005). The brain's concepts: The role of the sensorymotor system in conceptual knowledge. *Cognitive Neuropsychology*, 22, 455–479.

Gentileschi, V., Sperber, S., & Spinnler, H. (1999). Progressive defective recognition of familiar people. *Neurocase*, 5, 407–424.

Goodale, M. A. & Milner, A. D. (1992). Separate visual pathways for perception and action. *Trends Neuroscience*, 15, 20–25.

Goodale, M. A. & Milner, A. D. (2004). *Sight unseen: An exploration of conscious and unconscious vision.* Oxford: Oxford University Press.

Gorno-Tempini, M. L., Rankin, K. P., Woolley, J. D., Rosen, H. J., Phengrasamy, L., & Miller, B. L. (2004). Cognitive and behavioural profile in a case of right anterior temporal lobe neurodegeneration. *Cortex*, 40, 631–644.

Grabowski, T. J., Damasio, H., Tranel, D., Ponto, L. L., Hichwa, R. D., & Damasio, A. R. (2001). A role for the left temporal pole in the retrieval of words for unique entities. *Human Brain Mapping*, 13, 199–212.

Grabowski, T. J., Damasio, H., Tranel, D., Cooper, G. E., Ponto, L. L., Watkins, G. L., & Hichwa, R. D. (2003). Residual naming after damage to the left temporal pole: A PET activation study. *Neuroimage*, 19, 846–860.

Gracey, F. & Ownsworth, T. (2008).The self and identity in rehabilitation. *Neuropsychological Rehabilitation*, 18, 522–526.

Gracey, F. & Ownsworth, T. (2012). The experience of self in the world: The personal and social contexts of identity change after brain injury. In J. Jetten, C. Haslam & S. A. Haslam (Eds.), *The social cure: Identity, health and wellbeing* (pp. 273–295). Hove: Psychology Press.

Granerod, J. & Crowcroft, N. (2007). The epidemiology of acute encephalitis. In B.-K. Dewar & W. H. Williams (Eds.), *Encephalitis: Assessment and rehabilitation across the lifespan: Neuropsychological Rehabilitation Special Issue*, 17, 406–428.

Granerod, J., Cousens, S., Davies, N. W. S., Crowcroft, N. S., & Thomas, S. L. (2013). New estimates of incidence of encephalitis in England. *Emerging Infectious Diseases*, 19, 1455–1462.

Groh-Bordin, C. & Kerkoff, G. (2010). Recovery and treatment of sensory perceptual disorders. In J. M. Gurd, U. Kischka & J. C. Marshall (Eds.), *The handbook of clinical neuropsychology* 2nd edition (pp. 139–158). Oxford: Oxford University Press.

Hanley, J. R. & Kay, J. (1998). Proper name anomia and anomia for the names of people: Functionally dissociable impairments? *Cortex*, 34, 155–158.

Hanley, J. R. & Kay, J. (2010). Neuropsychological assessment and treatment of disorders of reading. In J. M. Gurd, U. Kischka & J. C. Marshall (Eds.), *The handbook of clinical neuropsychology* 2nd edition (pp. 296–322). Oxford: Oxford University Press.

Hanley, J. R., Young, A. W., & Pearson, N. (1989). Defective recognition of familiar people. *Cognitive Neuropsychology*, 6, 179–210.

Haslam, C., Holme, A., Haslam, S. A., Iyer, A., Jetten, J., & Williams, W. H. (2008). Maintaining group memberships: Social identity continuity predicts well-being after stroke. *Neuropsychological Rehabilitation*, 18, 671–691.

Haxby, J. V., Hoffman, E. A., & Gobbini, M. I. (2000). The distributed human neural system for face perception. *Trends in Cognitive Sciences*, 4, 223–233.

Hodges, S., Berry, E., & Wood, K. (2011). SenseCam: A wearable camera that stimulates and rehabilitates autobiographical memory. *Memory*, 19, 685–696.

Hokkanen. L. & Launes, J. (2007). Neuropsychological sequelae of acute-onset sporadic viral encephalitis. In B.-K. Dewar & W. H. Williams (Eds.), *Encephalitis: Assessment and rehabilitation across the lifespan: Neuropsychological Rehabilitation Special Issue*, 17, 450–477.

Hokkanen, L., Salonen, O., & Launes, J. (1996). Amnesia in acute herpetic and nonherpetic encephalitis. *Archives of Neurology*, 53, 972–978.

Hooper, L., Williams, W. H., Wall, S. E., & Chua, K.-C. (2007). Caregiver distress, coping and parenting styles in cases of childhood encephalitis. In B.-K. Dewar & W. H. Williams (Eds.), *Encephalitis: Assessment and rehabilitation across the lifespan: Neuropsychological Rehabilitation Special Issue*, 17, 621–637.

Humphreys, G. W. & Riddoch, M. J. (1987). *To see but not to see: A case study of visual agnosia.* Hillsdale, NJ: Lawrence Erlbaum Associates.

Humphreys, G. W. & Riddoch, M. J. (1988). On the case for multiple semantic systems: A reply to Shallice. *Cognitive Neuropsychology*, 5, 143–150.

Jackson, J. H. (1876). Case of large cerebral tumour without optic neuritis, and with left hemiplegia and imperception. *Royal London Ophthalmic Hospital Reports*, 8, 434–444.

James, W. (1880). *The principles of psychology* Vol. 1. New York, NY: Doer Publications.

James, W. (1890). *The principles of psychology*. Michigan: H. Holt.

Jennett, B. & Bond, M. (1975). Assessment of outcome after severe brain damage. *The Lancet*, 1(7905), 480–484.

Jetten, J., Haslam, C., & Haslam, S. A. (2012). *The social cure: Identity, health and well-being*. New York, NY: Psychology Press.

Joubert, S., Felician, O., Barbeau, E., Sontheimer, A., Barton, J. J., Ceccaldi, M., & Poncet, M. (2003). Impaired configurational processing in a case of progressive prosopagnosia associated with predominant right temporal lobe atrophy. *Brain*, 126, 2537–2550.

Joubert, S., Felician, O., Barbeau, E., Sontheimer, A., Guedj, E., Ceccaldi, M., & Poncet, M. (2004). Progressive prosopagnosia: clinical and neuroimaging results. *Neurology*, 63, 1962–1965.

Kanwisher, N., Tong, F., & Nakayama, K. (1998). The effect of face inversion on the human fusiform face area. *Cognition*, 68, B1–B11.

Kaplan, E., Goodglass, H., & Weintraub, S. (1983). *The Boston Naming Test*. Philadelphia, PA: Lea & Febiger.

Kapur, N., Barker, S., Burrows, E. H., Ellison, D., Brice, J., Illis, L. S., . . . Loates, M. (1994). *Herpes simplex* encephalitis: Long term magnetic resonance imaging and neuropsychological profile. *Journal of Neurology, Neurosurgery, and Psychiatry*, 57, 1334–1342.

Kartsounis, L. (2010). Assessment of perceptual disorders. In J. M. Gurd, U. Kischka & J. C. Marshall (Eds.), *The handbook of clinical neuropsychology* 2nd edition (pp. 120–138). Oxford: Oxford University Press.

Kay, J., Lesser, R., & Coltheart, M. (1996). Psycholinguistic assessments of language processing in aphasia: An introduction. *Aphasiology*, 10, 159–180.

Kennerknecht, I., Grueter, T., Welling, B., Wentzek, S., Horst, J., Edwards, S., & Grueter, M. (2006). First report of prevalence of non-syndromic hereditary prosopagnosia (HPA). *American Journal of Medical Genetics*, 140, 1617–1622.

Kennerknecht, I., Ho, N. Y., & Wong, V. C. N. (2008). Prevalence of hereditary prosopagnosia (HPA) in Hong Kong Chinese population. *American Journal of Medical Genetics*, 146, 2863–2870.

Kertesz, A. (1979). Visual agnosia: The dual deficit of perception and recognition. *Cortex*, 15, 403–419.

Kitchener, E. G. & Hodges, J. R. (1999). Impaired knowledge of famous people end events with intact autobiographical memory in a case of progressive right temporal degeneration: Implications for the organisation of remote memory. *Cognitive Neuropsychology*, 16, 589–607.

Klonoff, P. (2010). *Psychotherapy after brain injury principles and techniques.* New York, NY: Guilford Press.

Kolb, B. (1995). *Brain plasticity and behaviour.* Hillsdale, NJ: Lawrence Erlbaum Associates.

Kopelman, M. D., Stanhope, N., & Kingsley, D. (1999). Retrograde amnesia in patients with diencephalic, temporal lobe or frontal lesions. *Neuropsychologia*, 37, 939–958.

Lambon, R. M. A., Graham, K. S., Patterson, K., & Hodges, J. R. (1999). Is a picture worth a thousand words? Evidence from concept definitions by patients with semantic dementia. *Brain and Language*, 70, 309–335.

Larner, A. J. (2004). Lewis Carroll's Humpty Dumpty: An early report of prosopagnosia. *Journal of Neurology, Neurosurgery, and Psychiatry*, 75, 1063.

Laws, K. & Sartori, G. (2005). Category deficits and paradoxical dissociations in Alzheimer's disease and *Herpes simplex* encephalitis. *Journal of Cognitive Neuroscience*, 17, 1453–1459.

Leake, J. A., Albani, S., Kao, A., Senac, M. O., Billman, G. F., Nespeca, M. P., . . . J. S. Bradley. (2004). Acute disseminated encephalomyelitis in childhood: Epidemiologic, clinical and laboratory features. *Pediatric Infectious Diseases Journal*, 23, 756–764.

LeGrand, R., Cooper, P. A., Mondloch, C. J., Lewis, T. L., Sagiv, N., de Gelder, B., . . . Maurer, D. (2006). What aspects of face processing are impaired in developmental prosopagnosia? *Brain and Cognition*, 61, 139–158.

Levack, W. M. M., Kayes, N. M., & Fadyl, J. K. (2010). Experience of recovery and outcome following traumatic brain injury: A metasynthesis of qualitative research. *Disability & Rehabilitation*, 32, 986–999.

Lissauer, H. (1890). Ein Fall von Seelenblindheit nebst einem beitrage zue Theorie derselben. *Archiv fur Psychiatrie und Nervenkrankheiten*, 21, 22–270. [English translation by Jackson M. Lissauer on agnosia. *Cognitive Neuropsychology* (1988), 5, 155–192.]

Locke, J. & Winkler, K. (1996). *An essay concerning human understanding.* Indianapolis, IN: Hackett Publishing Company.

Markus, H. & Nurius, P. (1986). Possible selves. *American Psychologist*, 41, 954–969.

Marshall, J. F. (1985). Neural plasticity and recovery of function after brain injury. *International Review of Neurobiology*, 26, 201–247.

Maurer, D., Le Grand, R., & Mondloch, C. J. (2002). The many faces of configural processing. *Trends in Cognitive Sciences*, 6, 258–260.

McCarthy, R. A. & Warrington, E. K. (1986). Visual associative agnosia: A clinico-anatomical study of a single case. *Journal of Neurology, Neurosurgery and Psychiatry*, 49, 1233–1240.

McCarthy, R. A. & Warrington, E. K. (1988). Evidence for modality-specific meaning systems in the brain. *Nature*, 334, 428–430.

McCarthy, R. A. & Warrington, E. K. (1990). *Cognitive neuropsychology.* London: Academic Press.

McCarthy, R. A., Evans, J. J., & Hodges, J. R. (1996). Topographical amnesia: Spatial memory disorder, perceptual dysfunction, or category specific semantic memory impairment? *Journal of Neurology, Neurosurgery and Psychiatry*, 60, 318–325.

McClelland, J. L. (1981). Retrieving general and specific information from stored knowledge of specifics. *Proceedings of the Third Annual Meeting of the Cognitive Science Society*, 170–172.

McConachie, H. R. (1976). Developmental prosopagnosia. A single case report. *Cortex*, 12, 76–82.

McDonald, S., Flanagan, S., Rollins, J., & Kinch, J. (2003). TASIT: A new clinical tool for assessing social perception after traumatic brain injury. *The Journal of Head Trauma Rehabilitation*, 18, 219–238.

McKenna, K., Cooke, D. M., Fleming, J., Jefferson, A., & Ogden, S. (2006). The incidence of visual perceptual impairment in patients with severe traumatic brain injury. *Brain Injury*, 20, 507–518.

McNeil, J. E. & Warrington, E. K. (1993). Prosopagnosia: A face specific disorder. *Quarterly Journal of Experimental Psychology: Human Experimental Psychology*, 46, 1–10.

Miotto, E. (2007). Cognitive rehabilitation of amnesia after virus encephalitis: A case report. In B.-K. Dewar & W. H. Williams (Eds.), *Encephalitis: Assessment and rehabilitation across the lifespan: Neuropsychological Rehabilitation Special Issue*, 17, 551–566.

Mondini, S. & Semenza, C. (2006). How Berlusconi keeps his face: A neuropsychological study in a case of semantic dementia. *Cortex*, 42, 332–335.

Mondloch, C. J., Pathman, T., Le Grand, R., & Maurer, D. (2003). *Can children's insensitivity to spacing among facial features be attributed to immaturity in holistic processing?* Paper presented at the Annual Meeting of the Brain, Behavior and Cognitive Sciences Society, Ontario, Canada.

Naylor, E. & Clare, L. (2008). Awareness of memory functioning, autobiographical memory and identity in early-stage dementia. *Neuropsychological Rehabilitation*, 18, 590–606.

Nochi, M. (1997). Dealing with the "Void": Traumatic brain injury as a story. *Disability & Society*, 12, 533–555.

O'Connor, M., Butters, N., Militois, P., Eslinger, P., & Cermak, L. (1992). The dissociation of anterograde and retrograde amnesia in a patient with herpes encephalitis. *Journal of Clinical and Experimental Psychology*, 14, 159–178.

Orth, U., Trzesniewski, K. H., & Robins, R. W. (2010). Self-esteem development from young adulthood to old age: A cohort-sequential longitudinal study. *Journal of Personality and Social Psychology*, 98, 645–658.

Ownsworth, T. (2013). *The "old" and "new" me: Understanding changes to self after brain injury*. Talk presented at the Fifteenth Anniversary Conference of the Oliver Zangwill Centre, Newmarket, Suffolk, June 2013.

Ownsworth, T. (2014). *Self-identity after brain injury*. Hove: Psychology Press.

Pancaroglu, R., Busigny, T., Johnston, S., Sekunov, A., Duchaine, B., & Barton, J. J. S. (2011). The right anterior temporal lobe variant of prosopagnosia. *Journal of Vision*, 11, 573.

Pewter, S. M., Williams, W. H., Haslam, C., & Kay, J. M. (2007). Neuropsychological and psychiatric profiles in acute encephalitis in adults. In B.-K. Dewar & W. H. Williams (Eds.), *Encephalitis: Assessment and rehabilitation across the lifespan: Neuropsychological Rehabilitation Special Issue*, 17, 478–505.

Powell, J., Letson, S., Davidoff, J., Valentine, T., & Greenwood, R. (2008). Enhancement of face recognition learning in patients with brain injury using three cognitive training procedures. *Neuropsychological Rehabilitation*, 18, 182–203.

Prigatano, G. P. (1999). *Principles of neuropsychological rehabilitation.* New York, NY: Oxford University Press.

Pylyshyn, Z. W. (1973). What the mind's eye tells to the mind's brain: A critique of mental imagery. *Psychological Bulletin*, 80, 1–24.

Quaglino, A., Borelli, G. B., Della Sala, S., & Young, A. W. (2003). Quaglino's 1867 case of prosopagnosia. *Cortex*, 39, 533–540.

Ribot, T. (1881). *Les maladies de la memoire.* New York, NY: Appleton-Century Crofts.

Robertson, I. H. (1996). *Goal management training: A clinical manual.* Cambridge: PsyConsult.

Robson, P. (1989). Development of a new self-report questionnaire to measure self esteem. *Psychological Medicine*, 19, 513–518.

Rossion, B. (2014). Understanding face perception by means of prosopagnosia and neuroimaging. *Frontiers in Bioscience (Elite Ed.)*, 1, 258–307.

Sacchett, C. & Humphreys, G. W. (1992). Calling a squirrel a squirrel but a canoe a wigwam: A category-specific deficit for artefactual objects and body parts. *Cognitive Neuropsychology*, 9, 73–86.

Schmalzl, L., Palermo, R., & Coltheart, M. (2008a). Cognitive heterogeneity in genetically based prosopagnosia: A family study. *Journal of Neuropsychology*, 2, 99–117.

Schmalzl, L., Palermo, R., Green, M., Brunsdon, R., & Coltheart, M. (2008b). Training of familiar face recognition and visual scan paths for faces in a child with congenital prosopagnosia. *Cognitive Neuropsychology*, 25, 704–729.

Snowden, J., Griffiths, H., & Neary, D. (1994). Semantic dementia: Autobiographical contribution to preservation of meaning. *Cognitive Neuropsychology*, 11, 265–288.

Snowden, J. S., Thompson, J. C., & Neary, D. (2004). Knowledge of famous faces and names in semantic dementia. *Brain*, 127, 860–872.

Sparr, S. A., Jay, M., Drislane, F. W., & Venna, N. (1991). A historic case of visual agnosia revisited after 40 years. *Brain*, 114, 789–800.

Spillmann, L., Laskowski, W., Lange, K. W., Kasper, E., & Schmidt, D. (2000). Stroke-blind for colors, faces, and locations: Partial recovery after three years. *Restorative Neurology and Neuroscience*, 17, 89–103.

Stapley, S., Atkins, K., & Easton, A. (2009). *Acquired brain injury in adults (post encephalitis): A guide for primary and community care.* Malton: The Encephalitis Society.

Starza-Smith, A., Talbot, E., & Grant, C. (2007). Encephalitis in children: a clinical neuropsychology perspective. *Neuropsychological Rehabilitation*, 17, 506–527.

Stone, M. J. & Hawkins, C. (2007). A medical overview of encephalitis. In B.-K. Dewar & W. H. Williams (Eds.), *Encephalitis: Assessment and rehabilitation across the lifespan: Neuropsychological Rehabilitation Special Issue*, 17, 429–449.

Tajfel, H. & Turner, J. (1979). An integrative theory of intergroup conflict. In W. G. Austin & S. Worchel (Eds.), *The social psychology of intergroup relations* (pp. 33–48). Monterey, CA: Brooks-Cole.

Tanaka, Y., Miyazawa, Y., Hashimoto, R., Nakano, I., & Obayashi, T. (1999). Postencephalitic focal retrograde amnesia after bilateral anterior temporal lobe damage. *Neurology*, 22, 344–350.

Teuber, H.-L. (1968). Alteration of perception and memory in man. In L. Weiskrantz (Ed.), *Analysis of Behaviour Change*. New York, NY: Harper & Row.

Thompson, S. A., Graham, K. S., Williams, G., Patterson, K., Kapur, N., & Hodges, J. R. (2004). Dissociating person-specific from general semantic knowledge: Roles of the left and right temporal lobes. *Neuropsychologia*, 42, 359–370.

Tranel, D. (2006). Impaired naming of unique landmarks is associated with left temporal polar damage. *Neuropsychology*, 20, 1–10.

Tranel, D., Damasio, H., & Damasio, A. R. (1997). A neural basis for the retrieval of conceptual knowledge. *Neuropsychologia*, 35, 1319–1327.

Utley, T. F., Ogden, J. A., & Gibb, A. (1997). The long-term neuropsychological outcome of herpes simplex encephalitis in a series of unselected survivors. *Neuropsychiatry Neuropsychology & Behavioral Neurology*, 10(3), 180–189.

Valentine, T., Powell, J., Davidoff, J., Letson, S., & Greenwood, R. (2006). Prevalence and correlates of face recognition impairments after acquired brain injury. *Neuropsychological Rehabilitation*, 16, 272–297.

Warrington, E. K. & James, M. (1991). *The visual object and space perception battery*. Bury St Edmunds: Thames Valley Test Company.

Warrington, E. K. & Shallice, T. (1979). Semantic access dyslexia. *Brain*, 102, 43–63.

Warrington, E. K. & Shallice, T. (1984). Category specific semantic impairments *Brain*, 107, 829–854.

Wearing, D. (2005). *Forever today: A memoir of love and amnesia*. London: Doubleday.

Wigan, A. L. (1844). *The duality of the mind*. London: Longman.

Williams, H. L., Conway, M. A., & Cohen, G. (2008). Autobiographical memory. In G. Cohen & M. A. Conway (Eds.), *Memory in the real world* 3rd edn (pp. 21–90). Hove: Psychology Press.

Wilson, A. E. & Ross, M. (2003). The identity function of autobiographical memory: Time is on our side. *Memory*, 11(2), 137–149.

Wilson, B. A. (1997). Semantic memory impairments following non-progressive brain damage: A study of four cases. *Brain Injury*, 11, 259–269.

Wilson, B. A. (1999). *Case studies in neuropsychological rehabilitation*. New York, NY: Oxford University Press.

Wilson B. A. (2009). *Memory rehabilitation: Integrating theory and practice*. New York, NY: Guilford Press.

Wilson, B. A. & Bainbridge, K. (2013). Recovery takes time so don't give up. In B. A. Wilson, J. Winegardner, & F. Ashworth (Eds.), *Life after brain injury: Survivors' stories* (pp. 50–62). London: Psychology Press.

Wilson, B. A. & Claire (2013). A face is not a person. In B. A. Wilson, J. Winegardner & F. Ashworth (Eds.), *Life after brain injury: Survivors' stories* (pp. 98–109). London: Psychology Press.

Wilson, B. A. & Davidoff, J. (1993). Partial recovery from visual object agnosia: A 10 year follow-up study. *Cortex*, 29, 529–542.

Wilson, B. A., Baddeley, A. D., & Kapur, N. (1995). Dense amnesia in a professional musician following *herpes simplex* virus encephalitis. *Journal of Clinical and Experimental Psychology*, 17, 668–681.

Wilson, B. A., Clare, L., Young, A., & Hodges, J. (1997). Knowing where and knowing what: A double dissociation. *Cortex*, 33, 529–541.

Wilson, B. A., Kopelman, M., & Kapur, N. (2008). Prominent and persistent loss of self-awareness in amnesia: Delusion, impaired consciousness or coping strategy? *Neuropsychological Rehabilitation*, 18, 527–540.

Wilson, B. A., Evans, J. J., Gracey, F., & Bateman, A. (2009). *Neuropsychological rehabilitation: Theory, models, therapy and outcomes*. Cambridge: Cambridge University Press.

Wilson, B. A., Winegardner, J., & Ashworth, F. (Eds.) (2013). *Life after brain injury: Survivors' stories*. London: Psychology Press.

Wright, J. C. & Telford, R. (1996). Psychological problems following minor head injury: A prospective study. *British Journal of Clinical Psychology*, 35, 399–412.

Yardley, L., McDermott, L., Pisarski, S., Duchaine, B., & Nakayama, K. (2008). Psychosocial consequences of developmental prosopagnosia: A problem of recognition. *Journal of Psychosomatic Research*, 65, 445–451.

Young, A. W., Hellawell, D., & De Haan, E. H. F. (1988). Cross-domain semantic priming in normal subjects and a prosopagnosic patient. *The Quarterly Journal of Experimental Psychology Section A: Human Experimental Psychology*, 40, 561–580.

Zhen, Z., Fang, H., & Liu, J. (2013). The hierarchical brain network for face recognition. *PloS One*, 8, e59886.

Zihl, J. (2011). *Rehabilitation of visual disorders after brain injury* 2nd edition. Hove: Psychology Press.

Zihl, J. & Kennard, C. (1996). Disorders of higher visual functions. In T. Brandt, L. R. Caplan, J. Dichgans, H. C. Diener, & C. Kennard (Eds.), *Neurological disorders, course and treatment* (pp. 201–212). San Diego, CA: Academic Press.

Zoltan, B. (2007). *Vision, perception and cognition: A manual for the evaluation and treatment of the adult with acquired brain injury* 4th edition. Thoroughfare, NJ: Slack Inc.

Index